Improving Healthcare with Control Charts

Basic and Advanced SPC Methods and Case Studies

Also available from ASQ Quality Press:

Measuring Quality Improvement in Healthcare: A Guide to Statistical Process Control Applications
Raymond G. Carey, PhD and Robert C. Lloyd, PhD

How to Use Patient Satisfaction Data to Improve Healthcare Quality
Ralph Bell, PhD and Michael J. Krivich, CHE

Customer Driven Healthcare: QFD for Process Improvement and Cost Reduction
Ed Chaplin, MD, and John Terninko, PhD

Measuring Customer Satisfaction
Bob E. Hayes

Healthcare Performance Measurement: Systems Design and Evaluation
Vahe Kazandjian

Stop Managing Costs: Designing Healthcare Organizations around Core Business Systems
James P. Mozena, Charles E. Emerick, and Steven C. Black

Insights to Performance Excellence in Health Care: An Inside Look at the Baldrige Criteria for Health Care
Mark L. Blazey, Joel H. Ettinger, Paul Grizzell, and Linda Janczak

IWA-1:2001—Quality Management Systems: Guidelines for Process Improvements in Health Service Organizations
ISO/AIAG/ASQ

To request a complimentary catalog of ASQ Quality Press publications, call 800-248-1946, or visit our Web site at http://qualitypress.asq.org .

Improving Healthcare with Control Charts

Basic and Advanced SPC Methods and Case Studies

Raymond G. Carey

ASQ Quality Press
Milwaukee, Wisconsin

Improving Healthcare with Control Charts: Basic and Advanced SPC Methods and Case Studies
Raymond G. Carey

Library of Congress Cataloging-in-Publication Data

Carey, Raymond G.
  Improving healthcare with control charts : basic and advanced SPC methods and case
studies / Raymond G. Carey ; with guest author Larry V. Staker.
    p. cm.
  Includes bibliographical references and index.
  ISBN 0-87389-562-2
  1. Medical care—Quality control—Charts, diagrams, etc. 2. Process control—Statistical
methods. I. Staker, Larry V. II. Title.
  [DNLM: 1. Quality control. 2. Quality Assurance, Health Care—methods.
  3. Models, Statistical. W 84.1 C2751 2002]
  RA399.A1C363 2002
  362.1'068'5—dc21   2002011572

10 9 8 7 6 5 4 3 2

ISBN 0-87389-562-2

Publisher: William A. Tony
Acquisitions Editor: Annemieke Koudstaal
Project Editor: Craig S. Powell
Production Administrator: Gretchen Trautman
Special Marketing Representative: David Luth

ASQ Mission: The American Society for Quality advances individual, organizational, and
community excellence worldwide through learning,
quality improvement, and knowledge exchange.

Attention Bookstores, Wholesalers, Schools, and Corporations: ASQ Quality
Press books, videotapes, audiotapes, and software are available at quantity discounts with bulk
purchases for business, educational, or instructional use.
For information, please contact ASQ Quality Press at 800-248-1946, or write to ASQ Quality
Press, P.O. Box 3005, Milwaukee, WI 53201-3005.

To place orders or to request a free copy of the ASQ Quality Press Publications Catalog, including
ASQ membership information, call 800-248-1946. Visit our Web site at www.asq.org or
http://qualitypress.asq.org .

Printed in the United States of America

 Printed on acid-free paper

Quality Press
600 N. Plankinton Avenue
Milwaukee, Wisconsin 53203
Call toll free 800-248-1946
Fax 414-272-1734
www.asq.org
http://qualitypress.asq.org
http://standardsgroup.asq.org
E-mail: authors@asq.org

This book is dedicated to those physicians, nurses, and healthcare professionals who care enough about their patients that they never tire of trying to learn from their own data how to improve their care—and also to Dr. Don Berwick, who has shown his personal compassion and concern for my wife and other patients who have suffered at the hands of those who should have relieved their pain.

Table of Contents

List of Exhibits, Tables, and Figures

Acknowledgments

I would like to acknowledge the assistance of those who directly or indirectly helped me in the development of the theory and case studies presented in this book. Foremost among these are Lloyd Provost and Sandra Murray, who encouraged me to write this book and to whom I am indebted for their insights into SPC theory.

I am also grateful to those who reviewed various drafts of this book and offered suggestions to clarify and strengthen my writing. First among these reviewers is Dr. James Levett, the former chair of surgery at Lutheran General Hospital/Advocate (Park Ridge, Illinois). He was especially helpful in making suggestions on the case studies from the viewpoint of a physician who is knowledgable in the use of control charts. I also received invaluable suggestions on my explanation of SPC theory from Michael J. Cleary, PhD and Gordon K. Constable, PhD, both professors emeritus from Wright State University, Dayton, Ohio.

Words are not enough to thank Dr. Larry Staker, who in spite of an unbelievably heavy schedule accepted my invitation to write a chapter on his use of run and control charts in clinical practice. His contribution was critical to any book that hoped to show physicians how invaluable SPC could be for improving individual patient care.

Finally, I am grateful to my wife, Rita, who did not complain when I spent many hours alone on my computer and who emphasized the importance of using language that would be less technical and more understandable to healthcare professionals.

Raymond G. Carey

Preface

The fact that you are reading this page says something about you. It says not only that you are interested in improving healthcare, but that you are looking for better ways to implement changes and evaluate them.

You may already be familiar with the help that statistical process control (SPC) methodology can give you in attaining these goals. However, you may be struggling with one or more of the following problems:

- I am drowning in a sea of data. How do I begin to learn from it?

- Where do I focus to get the most out of my improvement efforts?

- How can I learn about the impact of various treatment methods on patient outcomes?

- I have made some changes, but how can I really know they are improvements?

- How can I measure the impact of improvement efforts on patient satisfaction?

- Why do we need so many types of control charts? How do I choose the best one for my situation?

- What's wrong with just looking at aggregated data before and after an intervention? Why should I use a run or control chart instead?

- How can we get the board members to focus on the long-term trends in performance data, and not just on last month's results?

- How can control charts be used to improve the quality of report card data?

- What are the differences between confidence limits and control limits? Between "outliers" and "special causes"?

On the other hand, perhaps you have never used SPC, but are wondering whether it has value for your particular situation. For example, you may be asking:

- What are SPC methods and how can they really help me improve healthcare?

- As a physician, can I use control charts in my practice?

- As a member of a board or an oversight committee, how can I use control charts to monitor key processes and outcomes?

- Can long-term care facilities use control charts to make sense out of the minimum data set (MDS) data?

- Do SPC methods, including control charts, have value for health plans and HMOs?

- How and why does the Joint Commission use control charts in their accreditation surveys?

If you can relate to any of the above problems or questions, this book is for you.

The author wants to share his passion for learning from data with you. He knows that SPC, when properly used, can help you learn effectively and efficiently from your data. The good news is that SPC is not as complicated as some might think. You do not have to become a statistician to effectively use SPC methods in your work. Nor do you require a significant expenditure of resources.

WHAT IS SPC?

Statistical process control (SPC) is a philosophy, a strategy, and a set of methods for ongoing improvement of systems, processes, and outcomes. The SPC approach is based on learning through data and has its foundation in the theory of variation (understanding common and special causes). The SPC strategy incorporates the concepts of an analytic study, process thinking, prevention, stratification, stability, capability, and prediction. SPC incorporates measurement, data collection methods, and planned experimentation. Graphical methods, such as Shewhart charts (more commonly called "control charts"), run charts, frequency plots, histograms, Pareto analysis, scatter diagrams, and flow diagrams are the primary tools used in SPC.

WHY WRITE ANOTHER BOOK ON SPC FOR HEALTHCARE?

I have written this book for several reasons:

- SPC has great potential to help us learn and improve in healthcare

- The use of SPC methodology in healthcare is increasing and definitely here to stay

- The few books explaining the theory and applications of SPC to healthcare are basic in theoretical content and limited in scope

- There are a number of misconceptions about the use of SPC in the healthcare industry that I would like to clear up

The use of SPC methods in healthcare has been increasing since 1990. One reason for this growth is that healthcare associations have begun to present seminars and workshops on SPC. For example, the Institute for Healthcare Improvement (IHI) in Boston has stressed the importance of viewing and analyzing data in a time-ordered design when the intent is to measure for improvement. Indeed, the IHI's annual forums on quality improvement have included seminars and workshops on SPC every year since 1991.

The Joint Commission on Accreditation of Healthcare Organizations (JCAHO) provided another major impetus to SPC when it announced its intention to use statistical process control methods in its 1998 accreditation guidelines. JCAHO began including control charts along with comparison charts beginning in its accreditation surveys in 2001. An article in the February 2002 issue of their *Journal on Quality Improvement*[1] explains their use of control charts in detail. Another article in the March 2002 issue explains their use of comparison charts.

Another reason for the increased attention to SPC may be the influence of trustees and directors of healthcare organizations who come from the field of manufacturing. Manufacturing firms commonly use SPC both for improving processes and for reporting key business measures.

Where will healthcare providers obtain the needed information about SPC? Managers in industry and manufacturing have many excellent textbooks and manuals to guide their efforts. Walter A. Shewhart, who developed SPC methodology in the 1920s to help AT&T make better phones, wrote what has become the "bible" for SPC users, *Economic Control of Quality of Manufactured Product,* in 1931. More recently, a number of outstanding textbooks on SPC have been written to help managers in manufacturing apply Shewhart's concepts to their processes. Among the most prominent authors are Douglas Montgomery (1991), Eugene Grant and Richard Leavenworth (1988), Donald Wheeler and David Chambers (1992), and Acheson J. Duncan (1986). Two well-written textbooks applying Deming's theory to manufacturing and some service industries are *Quality Improvement through Planned Experimentation* (1999) by Moen, Nolan, and Provost, and *The Improvement Guide* (1996) by Langley et al. In addition to these heavy textbooks, others have worked to simplify Shewhart's theory to help the average industrial worker use Shewhart's control charts for continuous quality improvement. Notable in this group are the books by Thomas Pyzdek (1990, 1992).

However, while these texts are excellent for use in industry, they have limited use for healthcare. One cannot merely transplant Shewhart's methods into healthcare without some modifications. In an effort to apply SPC to healthcare in a way that physicians and nurses would more easily understand, I co-authored *Measuring Quality Improvement in Healthcare: A Guide to Statistical Process Control Applications* (2001) with my associate at the time, Dr. Robert Lloyd. This book was based on my experiences as vice president of quality measurement at Lutheran General Hospital

(Park Ridge, Illinois). The book used a case study approach to teach healthcare providers how to choose the appropriate control chart and how to manage with the results. Soon afterward, Ballestracci and Barlow (1996) also published a book targeted at medical group practice to promote statistical thinking and to overcome what they referred to as "statistical illiteracy."

However, during the last 10 years I have consulted extensively with healthcare organizations both nationally and internationally. I found a good deal of confusion and misconceptions about the use of SPC in healthcare. I have listened to and tried to address in this volume the questions, problems, and puzzlement of physicians, nurses, and managers who have tried to improve quality through the implementation of SPC methods.

The principal audience I have in mind are those who already have some basic knowledge of the theory and tools of SPC and who want to move to a more advanced level. This book should be helpful to those who feel that they want to do more than use data as a Rorschach test, where everyone sees what they want to see in the data. It is addressed to those who want to collect and assess data about their own processes and systems in an economic way, so that they can learn where they need to improve and whether or not their improvement plans really were effective.

THE ORGANIZATION OF THIS BOOK

The content of part I is a review of the basic SPC theory and tools that were covered in my earlier book, although with some changes and modifications. I want to introduce a more simple process improvement plan with a clearer explanation of a run chart (chapter 1), as well as an improved control chart decision tree and a simplification of the tests for special causes (chapter 2).

Part II will introduce more advanced SPC concepts and methods. Chapter 3 presents a plan on how to drill down into aggregated data to improve a process. Chapter 4 addresses some difficult theoretical and practical problems regarding the construction and use of control charts. Chapter 5 discusses some of the limitations of attribute charts that tend to be overlooked and can lead to inaccurate conclusions from the data. Chapter 6 emphasizes the need to obtain meaningful data without which control charts are only "chart junk." It will address guidelines for developing indicators, sampling methods, benchmarking, and setting goals and targets. Case studies will be used throughout the chapters to illustrate the ideas under discussion. Readers are encouraged not to skip over a case study because the content is not focused on their specific situations or areas of interest. Rather, readers are encouraged to focus on the learning principles involved and how these principles might apply to their own circumstances and work areas.

Part III deals with some special applications of the SPC theory and methods discussed in parts I and II. Chapter 7 demonstrates how to use SPC to analyze patient survey data so that providers can learn from their data and improve care. The focus of chapter 8 is on how trustees can be more statistically sophisticated in analyzing data on the quality of care through the use of control charts, balanced scorecards, goal setting, and comparison data. Chapter 9 addresses the subject of Six Sigma both as a statistic and as a program. In what way is Six Sigma different from SPC? Does Six Sigma have a place in healthcare improvement? Chapter 10 was written by Dr. Larry Staker, chief medical officer of Deseret Mutual (Salt Lake City). He presents three case studies that demonstrate how run and control charts can and should be used in clinical practice to monitor and improve individual patient care.

ENDNOTE

1. K. Lee and C. McGreevey, "Using Control Charts to Assess Performance Measurement Data," *Journal on Quality Improvement* 28, no. 2 (2002): 90–101.

Introduction

Data collection and measurement are fundamental to SPC. Therefore, before reading the theory and case studies presented in this book, it may be useful to consider some of the emotional, political, and social issues that create the climate or culture in which measurement occurs. Hopefully these considerations will help you in your data collection efforts. I have grouped these ideas under the following headings:

- Why do some healthcare professionals find measuring quality a difficult task?
- Who wants to see healthcare quality measured?
- Why are different approaches to measurement needed?

WHY DO SOME HEALTHCARE PROFESSIONALS FIND MEASURING QUALITY A DIFFICULT TASK?

When you hear or see the word *measurement*, what feelings do you experience? It is not uncommon for people to experience a feeling of discomfort. They want to put the thought of measurement out of their minds quickly. Not many embrace measurement with enthusiasm. Why? There are many reasons. "Measurement" may bring back memories of school and report cards or of performance appraisals. In addition, healthcare processes and outcomes, like many of the important things in life, are hard to measure.

Physicians in general have been less than enthusiastic about measuring healthcare quality. Michael Millenson is a Pulitzer nominee and author of *Demanding Medical Excellence*, a book that former Surgeon General C. Everett Koop, MD, says should be read by everyone who has a stake in the quality of American medicine.

Millenson, in an interview for *Synergy* about his book, is quoted as saying: "I have been deeply disillusioned by the failure of the profession to respond to the scientific literature on quality of care improvement . . . the clear message is that, unless the financial incentives are aligned correctly, doctors will simply practice according to the medieval guild-like paradigm: I graduated from a good medical school. I work very hard, my patients mostly leave the office alive and happy, and therefore I'm giving high-quality care."[1] However, this view fails to take into consideration the pressures that have been put upon doctors in recent years, especially under managed care, to work with fewer resources, to give fewer tests, to see more patients and to be under increasingly public scrutiny regarding the care they provide. They have seen their work hours lengthened and their incomes reduced. In the face of this, they perceive that they are being asked to measure quality without the meaningful incentives to do so and with the concern that the data may be used against them.

WHO WANTS TO SEE HEALTHCARE QUALITY MEASURED?

There are a number of different constituencies who have a stake in wanting quality assessed. However, because they have different reasons for measuring quality, the same approach to measurement will not fit everyone's needs.

Purchasers of Care

First, there are the purchasers of care. Up until about 1995, their primary concern was cost. Understandably so. The rate of healthcare cost was increasing by as much as 18 percent annually. Large corporations were spending an ever-increasing percentage of their overhead on healthcare. For example, General Motors was spending more than one billion dollars a year on healthcare for their current or retired employees. General Electric spent just under one billion dollars a year. It is therefore not surprising that their first questions to health providers were: What are your per-member, per-month charges, and what is your expected annual rate of increase?

However, by 1994, under pressure from the threat of government intervention, healthcare costs increased less than two percent annually, with some variation by size of hospital and section of the country. In July 1995, Dr. Paul Ellwood, a pioneer in the development of health maintenance organizations (HMOs), convened a meeting in Jackson Hole, Wyoming that was attended by 30 officials of federal, state, and local employee organizations, consumer groups, and officials of such major employers as American Express, the Minnesota Mining and Manufacturing Company (3M), the Ameritech Corporation, and PepsiCo. Together they represented an estimated 80 million consumers of health insurance. The attendees agreed that they would play down cost issues and switch their priorities from cost to quality.[2] This change in priorities meant that the purchasers would no longer choose their health provider based only on cost considerations, but on value; that is, the quality of care they received for their healthcare dollars.

In 1999, an HMO in Ohio, Anthem Blue Cross and Blue Shield, released a year-long study to determine the best place for its insured patients to undergo heart surgery.[3] The study is narrow, looking only at heart-surgery operations at hospitals in Ohio. It did not measure everything that might be considered part of the "quality" of care, focusing mostly on heart-surgery deaths and "adverse outcomes" such as heart attack, strokes, and infections. The full results and methodology were not made public, but the results suggested that reputation and reality did not always match. Many hospitals did not like the results of the study, but the study has made it clear that the purchasers of care want to see more measurement of quality on the part of hospitals—not just testimonials and anecdotal evidence of quality. By the year 2002, the increase in the cost of healthcare was again on the rise. As a result, purchasers of care were even more motivated to know the quality of care they were getting for their healthcare dollar.

Accreditation Agencies

A second group of stakeholders is the accreditation agencies, such as the Joint Commission on Accreditation of Healthcare Organizations (JCAHO), located in Oakbrook, Illinois, and the National Committee on Quality Assurance (NCQA), located in Washington, D.C.

JCAHO has continuously modified its approach to measuring quality. During the 1980s, its approach was a process referred to as *quality assurance.* In addition to supervising the credentialling process, JCAHO expected hospitals to choose quality indicators from among high-volume and high-risk procedures and to specify "thresholds for evaluation." Hospitals were then expected to take action on problem areas or on people when the threshold was exceeded. In the early 1990s, JCAHO switched its focus to *quality improvement.* The Commission asked hospitals to identify areas where the delivery of care could be improved and to document the results of improvement efforts. The 1998 JCAHO standards introduced the concept of statistical process control to measure process improvement. Hospitals and other healthcare organizations were expected to submit data on self-selected indicators of care (given the name "ORYX indicators") to JCAHO. Using its own software program, JCAHO planned to identify opportunities for improvement by studying comparison data from similar healthcare organizations or through risk-adjusted data, and also to measure process improvement using control chart analysis. Beginning in 2001, JCAHO began to include control charts along with comparison charts as part of the pre-survey material sent to healthcare organizations in preparation for the accreditation survey. (See the articles in the February and March 2002 issues of the Joint Commission's *Journal on Quality Improvement.*)

In contrast, NCQA focuses on developing "report card" data that are intended to assist purchasers of care and the public at large to make comparisons among managed care providers. NCQA developed a set of indicators that are collectively referred to as the Health Plan Employer Data and Information Set, or HEDIS indicators. HEDIS is a set of standardized performance measures that is intended to assess the quality of health-care and services provided by managed care plans. These measures were developed in conjunction with public and private purchasers, health plans, researchers, and consumer advocates. At first, these were almost exclusively process indicators, such as the percent of HMO plan members who had immunizations or mammograms. Later some outcome measures were added. The HEDIS data are available at the NCQA Web site.

Governing Bodies

A third group of stakeholders is the governing bodies of healthcare facilities. They are legally responsible for monitoring the care provided. They need to identify areas of excellence, as well as opportunities for improvement. If they oversee an integrated health system, they need to know which facilities excel in the treatment of specific disease entities or in certain surgical procedures. They need to ascertain whether there are procedures or areas that put patients, hospitals, or providers at risk. To do this, trustees need some way to make valid comparative judgments about the quality of care. Merely having JCAHO or NCQA accreditation is not adequate for the Boards to make these judgments. In July 1999, a report released by the Department of Health and Human Services' inspector general stated that hospital regulators rely too much on trust and cooperation and not enough on tough enforcement. "They could not detect a flaw that the hospitals did not want them to detect," said George F. Grob, a deputy inspector general who oversaw the four-volume report.[4]

General Public

A fourth group of stakeholders is the general public. There may have been a time when most American felt that the United States had the best healthcare system in the world. Most gave their unquestioned trust to their physicians and the hospitals to which their physicians sent them. However, in recent years a growing number of articles raising questions about the quality of care in the United States have weakened this unquestioning trust. For example, the cover of *Time* magazine on January 22, 1996 pictured a doctor with a gag in his mouth together with a nine-page cover story about a mother's fight to survive cancer when her HMO forbade her physicians to prescribe a course of treatment that was covered by insurance. The *Chicago Tribune* printed a magazine insert in its Sunday edition with a story titled, "When Doctors Are the Problem,"[5] alleging that about 5% of physicians, or about 31,000, have at some time put their patients' health at risk. *The New York Times* published a story about a little boy in a Houston hospital who died because the child received 0.9 milligrams of digoxin instead of 0.09 milligrams. The attending doctor missed the error in the amount of the drug, and no physician, nurse, pharmacist, or technician corrected it.[6]

An article in the *Wall Street Journal* by Marilyn Chase concluded, "Managed care, at its best, has put the brakes on runaway inflation and curbed overuse—something doctors long failed to do. At its worst it has made a travesty of the phrase 'quality of care,' now the mantra of every cut-rate plan with a schmaltzy TV commercial."[7] This assessment is painful to read for providers and patients alike. However, the author highlighted two indisputable facts: first, the public is looking more and more for healthcare to provide documentation of claims of quality, and second, providers have not done an outstanding job of providing it.

Perhaps the most devastating of all was the report released in December 1999, by the Institute of Medicine (IOM), a branch of the National Academies, entitled: "To Err is Human." Many newspapers and journals gave this report high visibility. *Time* featured a story with pictures entitled "Doctors' Deadly Mistakes: Medical Errors Kill Up to 98,000 Americans Yearly."[8] The report also proposed a series of solutions, including a new Federal Center for Patient Safety that would set error-reduction standards for hospital procedures and medical equipment, as well as a mandatory reporting system that would require hospitals to report what are referred to as "adverse events." In 2001, IOM issued a follow-up report, *Crossing the Quality Chasm*. This report presented a more theoretical discussion of the meaning of quality, the components of quality, and how to build a quality organization.

Providers

A fifth group of stakeholders is the providers themselves. Among providers I include everyone connected with healthcare delivery: administrators, physicians, nurses, therapists, pharmacists, lab technicians, radiologists, and support staff. Providers may be facility-based or office-based, part of an organized delivery system and/or group practice.

Responsible providers are worried about the effect of curtailed healthcare resources on the care they provide. For example, Robert Brook, Caren Kamberg, and Elizabeth McGlynn challenged physicians to be concerned about the trade-off between cost and quality. They also cautioned physicians not to assume that they were providing quality care merely because they used procedures that were supported by solid basic research. They further explained that basic research shows only the efficacy of a procedure, not its effectiveness in actual practice. For example, they said that basic research demonstrates the efficacy of a carotid endarterectomy with patients who have a 70 percent to 99 percent occlusion of the carotid artery. However, when this procedure was used in community hospitals, the good effects that happened under controlled conditions did not always occur, and sometimes unwanted side effects, such as strokes, did. The challenge of caring physicians, therefore, is to adapt research to the real world of their practices and know whether the care they provide is improving or deteriorating as they make changes.[9]

These five groups of stakeholders are not intended to be mutually exclusive nor are they necessarily presented in the order of importance. For example, when members of the general public become patients, they might also be purchasers of care. Providers (physicians, nurses, administrators) might at times also act as agents of accreditation bodies. The intent here is to show that the need for measurement is broadly based and is grounded in sociologically diverse segments of the population.

WHY ARE DIFFERENT APPROACHES TO MEASUREMENT NEEDED?

Different audiences (or stakeholders) have different goals or purposes in mind when they gather data. The same approach will not work for all. For example, Figure I.1 presents three approaches to measuring quality: assembling report card data, conducting basic research, and using statistical process control (SPC) methodology. The proper choice depends on the audience for whom the data are collected and the purpose for which the data are collected.

Leif Solberg, Gordon Mosser, and Sharon McDonald from the Institute for Clinical Systems Integration in Minnesota explain, "We are increasingly realizing not only how critical measurement is to the quality improvement we seek, but how counterproductive it can be to mix measurement for accountability or research with measurement for improvement."[10] Classical statistics are useful to providers who need to know that their medical treatments are founded on solid basic research. However, classical statistics, which are taught in standard statistics courses, will not address every measurement need. Employers, insurers, and other purchasers of care want "report card" data to defend their choice of healthcare providers. Providers also need to know whether planned interventions, such as new clinical pathways and protocols, have had an adverse or positive effect on their processes and procedures in their own practices. In addition, hospital governance (boards of trustees) needs to monitor performance on an ongoing basis. For these purposes, classical statistics will not always work. SPC analysis is often a better choice.

The framework of three different approaches to measuring quality is meant to emphasize that no single approach to measurement fits all situations. Each is useful and necessary depending on the audience and specific purpose. Those interested in a more thorough discussion of the relationship between measuring for improvement and basic research might read the journal articles by Casarett, Karlawish, and Sugarman (2000)[11] and by Byers and Beaudin (2002).[12]

Approach	Audience	Purpose
Report card data	Insurers/Purchasers of care	Accountability/Judgment
Basic research	Physicians/Researchers	Efficacy of procedures or treatments
Statistical process control	All providers	Effectiveness of procedures/ Improvement of processes and outcomes
Statistical process control	Governance	Monitoring performance

Figure I.1   Three approaches to measuring quality.

ENDNOTES

1. M. L. Millenson, interview in *Synergy*, Physician/Hospital Institute (Spring 1999): 53.
2. "Quality in Focus for Health Plans," *New York Times*, 3 July 1995.
3. "HMO Rates Hospitals; Many Don't Like It, But They Get Better," *Wall Street Journal,* 22 April 1999.
4. As quoted in the *Chicago Tribune*, 21 July 1999.
5. B. Gavzer, "When Doctors Are the Problem," *Chicago Tribune,* 14 April 1996, Parade Section.
6. L. Belkin, "Who's to Blame? It's the Wrong Question," *New York Times Magazine*, 15 June 1997, sec. 6, 28–33.
7. *Wall Street Journal*, 24 November 1997, Health Journal, B1.
8. M. D. Lemonick, "Doctors' Deadly Mistakes: Medical Errors Kill Up to 98,000 Americans Yearly," *Time*, 13 December 1999, 74.
9. "Health System Reform and Quality," *Journal of the American Medical Association* 276, no.6 (14 August 1996): 476.
10. L. Solberg, G. Mosser, and S. McDonald, "The Three Faces of Performance Measurement: Improvement, Accountability, and Research," *Journal on Quality Improvement* 23, no.3 (March 1997): 135.
11. D. Casarett, J. H. Karlawish, and J. Sugarman, "Determining When Quality Improvement Initiatives Should Be Considered Research: Proposed Criteria and Potential Implications," *Journal of the American Medical Association* 283, no. 17 (2000): 2275–80.
12. J. F. Byers and C. L. Beaudin, "The Relationship between Continuous Quality Improvement and Research," *Journal of Healthcare Quality* (January/February 2002): 4–8.

Part I

Using Data for Improvement: Basic SPC Theory and Methods

1

Basic SPC Concepts and the Run Chart

L et us suppose for the moment that you are a hospital administrator. You have been asked whether you have meaningful data to show that patient care at your hospital is any better than it was a year ago. Has accessibility to care improved? Has pain management in the emergency department improved? Has patient safety as measured by the number of medical errors or patient falls improved? Has the percent of readmissions for congestive heart failure decreased? Has the percent mortality in heart surgery decreased? Is the success of your current "improvement plans" being assessed in a sound statistical manner?

This chapter will first describe some basic concepts in statistical thinking needed to develop an improvement plan to evaluate these questions. Second, it will describe a simple and economical tool to assist managers in effectively and validly assessing their improvement plans—namely, a run chart. Chapter 2 will describe the more sophisticated tool for accomplishing the same purpose—the control chart developed by Walter Shewhart.

A SIMPLE PROCESS IMPROVEMENT PLAN

In conducting basic research under laboratory conditions, it is possible to set up a treatment group and a control group and randomly assign patients to one or another group. By using parametric statistics, such as a t-test or analysis of variance, one can determine whether or not the treatment has had a statistically significant effect. Such a study is valuable to determine the *efficaciousness* of an intervention, but not its *effectiveness* under clinical conditions of practice.

Note: Major portions of this chapter appeared previously in the *Journal of Ambulatory Care Management* 25:1 (January 2002): 80–87, and are reprinted here with permission.

When patients come for care, we cannot randomly assign them to a physician, a care unit, or a mode of treatment. Yet we need to monitor our treatment processes and determine whether or not they are functioning at a consistent and acceptable level as measured by one or more criteria. Determining the effectiveness of our care under clinical conditions requires a different approach than that used in basic research. We have a single stream of data. Therefore, we need to develop a process improvement plan and measure the results differently than we would when conducting basic research under laboratory conditions.

The initial step is to develop a simple process improvement plan. This can be done by answering three questions:

1. What process should we try to improve?

2. How will we know that a change will be an improvement?

3. What change can we make to effect that improvement?

The first question can be answered in different ways: by listening to patient complaints; by listening to staff complaints; or by examining clinical, operational, or financial data. For example, why do patients complain? Because they have to wait too long to be scheduled for a lab or blood tests? Because the waiting time in the emergency department is too long? Because their interactions with physicians or therapists are unacceptable? Do physicians complain that it is taking too long to get the results of lab tests? Is the number of medical errors a cause for concern?

The second question regarding when a change will be an improvement requires some careful planning. We begin by asking what aspect of the identified process needs improvement. Some authors refer to this as the *key quality characteristic* (KQC). Others prefer the expression *key value indicator* (KVI). Others dislike the use of any acronyms and just ask: What aspect of a process are we trying to improve? For example, if patient safety is the process we wish to improve, what will be the aspect of safety we wish to improve? Patient falls? Medication errors? Misdiagnoses? If patient satisfaction is low, should we be focusing on improving accessibility to care? Or waiting time in the lab areas or in the emergency department?

After identifying a KQC of the process we wish to improve, it is *critical* to agree on the way in which we will *quantifiably* measure the KQC. Some refer to this as the *operational definition* of the KQC. For example, which definition of "patient fall" will we use so that consistent data can be gathered? How will we define a "medication error"? If we have identified office waiting time as a KQC, how will this be calculated? From the time of a patient's arrival until he or she is seen by the clinician? Or, from the time of the scheduled appointment until seen by the clinician?

Agreeing on the operational definition of the KQC that we want to improve is essential to obtaining reliable data. The aim of an operational definition is clear communication between everyone. A good operational definition creates a consistent meaning that everyone understands. It *reduces variability* in data collection. It is required for *all types* of data, and most importantly, it should be developed *before* data are gathered.

Before one concludes that an unstable control chart indicates an unstable process, operational definitions should be reviewed for validity. Has the definition changed? Is it still relevant to the process? Have the data collectors been adequately trained in applying the definition?

After identifying the KQC and operational definition with which data will be gathered, the final step in determining that a change made an improvement involves plotting data over time and analyzing the type of variation. This can be done in a straightforward manner with run or control charts. A run chart will be explained further on in this chapter. Control charts will be discussed in chapter 2.

The third step in the improvement plan is to determine which change we will make to effect an improvement. Identifying this change involves generating possible options, prioritizing the options, and then implementing them one at a time—measuring the effect of each in a trial-and-error approach. This is often referred to in statistical process control (SPC) terminology as the "plan–do–study–act" (PDSA) cycle, which will be explained later.

BEFORE AND AFTER MEASURES

It is not uncommon for an improvement team to measure the effect of an improvement effort by summarizing the average scores before and after the intervention and comparing the two numbers. If the results of a t-test or Chi-square showed the difference to be "statistically significant," they would conclude that the intervention (or change effort) was an improvement.

However, the only valid inference in comparing "before and after" scores is that one number has a high probability of being higher than the other! No valid conclusion can be drawn regarding the effect of an improvement plan without examining the *stability* of the processes that produced both summary statistics.

For example, suppose that a group of cardiac surgeons introduced a new protocol at the beginning of 1999 that was intended to reduce mortality for coronary artery bypass graft (CABG) surgery. The data from 1998 showed an overall mortality rate of 5 percent, while the data from 1999 showed a rate of 4 percent (see Figure 1.1). Should they celebrate this improvement in mortality rate? Obviously, a 20 percent reduction in mortality is clinically significant. What about statistical significance? If there were enough cases during these two years, a test for the difference between two proportions will be statistically significant, which merely means that the observed results could not have happened by chance. Let us also assume that the cases in both years were adjusted for severity, showing that the patients were approximately of the same age, the same gender, and with equal risk factors. However, the question often overlooked is: Are the processes that produced these two aggregate measures stable? If they are not, the comparisons based on summary statistics are invalid.

Now examine this process for stability by tracking the monthly mortality rates for the years 1998 and 1999 on a run chart (see Figure 1.2).

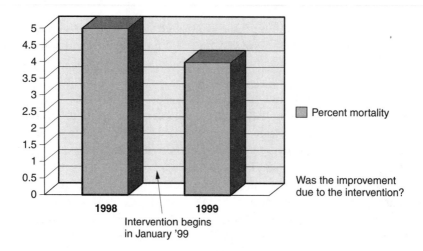

Figure 1.1   Average CABG mortality before and after implementation of new protocol.
Average mortality decreased from 5 percent to 4 percent.

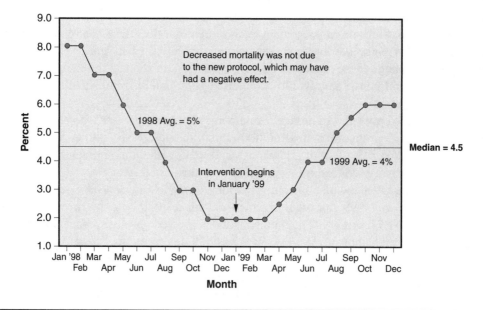

Figure 1.2   CABG mortality before and after new protocol.

The run chart rules for detecting the stability of the process (described later in this chapter) show that this process is clearly unstable and unpredictable. It has what is called *special cause variation*. Although the average rate decreased from 5 percent in 1998 to 4 percent in 1999, it was not due to the change effort, which may have had a negative effect. After the intervention in January 1999, the average monthly rate actually increased from 2 percent at the beginning 1998 to 6 percent by end of 1999. The lesson? Comparing aggregate data with summary statistics can be misleading unless the processes that produced the data are stable.

Therefore, what is the answer to this measurement problem? To test the effectiveness of a new procedure or protocol, providers will profit from using the SPC methodology originally developed by Walter A. Shewhart (1931) to help AT&T make better telephones, a methodology that since 1990 has become widely used in healthcare systems in the United States.

TYPES OF VARIATION

Shewhart theorized that the way to improve a process was to reduce variation and, when feasible, to move the entire process in the desired direction. However, he distinguished two types of variation: *assignable* and *unassignable* (more frequently referred to today as *special* and *common* cause variation). He taught that managers need to use a different approach to improve a process with common cause variation than one with special cause variation. He developed control charts to distinguish one type of variation from the other.

With common cause variation, the variation is inherent in the process itself. The process is stable and predictable within certain limits. Common cause variation is best described as "noise," or random variation, which can result from many factors inherent in a process. With special cause variation, one or more data points vary in an unpredictable manner from a cause not inherent in the process. This is a "signal" that the process has changed (either for better or worse).

Neither type of variation is good or bad in itself. When one did not plan for a special cause, it will usually be undesirable. When one makes a change to improve a process, a special cause can signal that the change effort has indeed been effective. On the other hand, a process that exhibits only common cause variation may be stable and predictable, but totally unacceptable. For example, a heart surgery mortality rate of 10 percent, plus or minus 5 percent, is a stable, but obviously unacceptable, rate.

How then should the type of variation determine management strategy? When a process exhibits *special* cause variation, the change effort should focus on investigating the origin of the special cause, and not on changing the process. For example, if the mortality rate for 10 months averaged 4 percent, with monthly averages varying slightly above or below 4 percent, this would suggest common cause variation. Then if the mortality rate in one month jumped to a 10 percent rate, the surgeons should not respond by changing their operative procedures (the process), but should first investigate the reason for the big jump in mortality for that month (the "special cause").

On the other hand, when a process exhibits only common cause variation but is functioning at an unacceptable level, management strategy should focus on reducing the amount of variation and moving the process average in the desired direction. This strategy involves implementing successive changes in the process and evaluating the effect of each change. This strategy is often referred to as the "plan–do–study–act," or PDSA, cycle:

1. *Plan* a change. This means modifying the current process in some way, or perhaps redesigning it completely.

2. *Do* it in a trial or on a small test group.

3. *Study* the results. Ask whether the new process has a level of performance and/or random variation that is superior to that displayed by the old process.

4. *Act.* Either implement the tested alternative, modify it and test again, or discard it.

If, in the above example, surgeons saw that their mortality rate was a *stable* process with a 4 percent average, but considered this rate *unacceptable*, then the surgeons should try to *change their process* by implementing and testing one or more changes in their surgical protocols.

THE RUN CHART

To assist managers in distinguishing common from special cause variation in their processes, Shewhart developed a tool called the *control* chart. The prototype of a control chart is called a *run* chart. Both are diagnostic tools to assist managers of a process in determining the type of variation. The run chart compared to a control chart is similar to an x-ray compared to an MRI test. An x-ray is less costly than an MRI, but is also less sensitive. Sometimes an x-ray will be adequate for the physician's need. For example, an x-ray will usually reveal whether or not a bone is broken, but not whether the patient has a slight tear in the rotator cuff or a hairline stress fracture.

A run chart is very simple to construct and interpret. It can be used with any process and with any type of data: measurement data, count data, percentages, ratios, and so on. On the other hand, there are several types of control charts. The choice among them is determined by the type of data (measurement data, count data, percentages, ratios, and so on). A run chart can be constructed with paper and pencil. It requires no statistics and is easily understood. Control charts are ordinarily constructed with the help of a computer software program. They also are a little more complex to interpret. In this chapter, I will explain and demonstrate only a run chart. In the following chapter I will explain and demonstrate the more sensitive tool—the control chart.

What Is a Run Chart?

Look back to the run chart in Figure 1.2, page 6. The run chart is a running record of a process over time. It is a different approach from merely comparing two aggregate measures, for example, 5 percent versus 4 percent mortality rate. The units of time by which the measurements are made (in this instance, months) are located on the *horizontal* axis. The aspect of the process being measured (the KQC) is on the *vertical* axis of the chart. (The horizontal axis is sometimes referred to as the "X" axis, and the vertical axis as the "Y" axis.) The centerline of the chart is the average score. With a run chart the average score is determined by the *median*, while the centerline of a control chart will be the arithmetic *mean* of all the points. Taking a sheet of paper and sliding it over the chart from the top down until half of the data points are above and half below the centerline can easily identify the median. In this case, with 24 points, there will be 12 points above and 12 below the median.

What Is a "Run"?

A *run* is defined as one or more consecutive data points on the same side of the median. A run could have a single point, or many points. In this chart, there are three runs. The first is a run of seven points in length. The second is 12 points in length. The third is five points in length.

What Are the Tests for a Special Cause?

There are a number of run chart tests to identify a special cause that can be found in textbooks. Usually three tests are adequate.

Test #1: The presence of too much or too little variability. When are there two few or too many runs? Table 1.1 displays a section of a probability chart developed by mathematicians.[1] It is not necessary to understand how it was developed. Just use it for reference purposes. Ordinarily, it is best to have at least 16 points in a run chart, excluding those on the median, to have adequate statistical *power* to identify a special cause. After 25 data points, additional data will not appreciatively increase the power of the tests.

In the run chart in Figure 1.2, there are 24 data points, but only three runs. Table 1.1 shows that with 24 points, if there are less than eight runs, it is a signal that one or more special causes are present.

Test #2: The presence of a shift in the process. A special cause exists if a run contains too many data points (that is, the run is too long). With 20 or more data points, a run of eight or more data points is "too long." (With less than 20 points, a run of seven might also be considered "too long.")

In Figure 1.2 the longest run is 12 points in length, also signaling the presence of a special cause, namely, a shift in the process.

Table 1.1   Probability table for run charts.

Number of Observations Excluding Points on the Median	Lower Limit for the Number of Runs	Upper Limit for the Number of Runs
14	4	11
15	4	12
16	5	12
17	5	13
18	6	13
19	6	14
20	6	15
21	7	15
22	7	16
23	8	16
24	**8**	**17**
25	9	17
26	9	18
27	9	19
28	10	19
29	10	20
30	11	21

Test #3: The presence of a trend. A *trend* is defined as an unusually long series of *consecutive* increases or decreases in the data. Experts disagree as to the exact number, but usually require that the number should be at least six or seven. The important lesson for healthcare managers is not to be "trend-happy," to be aware that three or four points are *not* to be considered a "trend." For this test, count any points on the median, but ignore points that repeat the preceding value. In Figure 1.2 there are two trends: each of seven in length. The first begins in January 1998 at 8 percent and ends in November 1998 at 2 percent. The second trend begins in March 1999 at 2 percent and ends in October 1999 at 6 percent.

CASE STUDY: REDUCING DELAYS FROM ABNORMAL MAMMOGRAM TO BIOPSY

The Situation

The medical director of the Worldbest Health Plan was concerned about what he felt were inordinate delays in the time between reading an abnormal mammogram and obtaining a definitive biopsy. He collected the average delay time per week for a period of 20 weeks (see Figure 1.3), presented them to a continuous quality improvement (CQI) team, and instructed them to remedy the problem. He felt an average waiting time

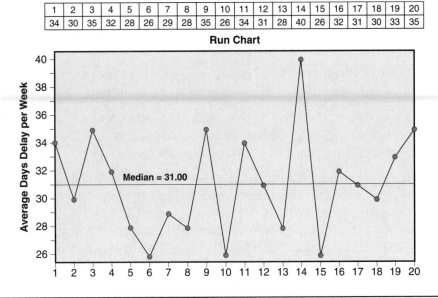

1	2	3	4	5	6	7	8	9	10	11	12	13	14	15	16	17	18	19	20
34	30	35	32	28	26	29	28	35	26	34	31	28	40	26	32	31	30	33	35

Figure 1.3　Average days from positive mammogram to definitive biopsy.

of 31 days was unacceptable. He also felt that the process was continuing to deteriorate. He pointed to the fact that the delay time reached 40 days during week 14. In addition, during the last six weeks he felt there was a "negative trend" from 26 days to 35 days of wait time.

Questions

1. Does this process show common or special cause variation?

2. Is the current process stable and predictable?

3. What should the team's strategy be to improve the process?

4. How will they know whether or not a planned change will be effective?

Analysis and Interpretation

1. None of the three run chart tests indicated the presence of a special cause.

   • There were a total of 18 points, excluding the two points that were exactly on the median. There were 13 runs. The probability table (Table 1.1) showed that with 18 points, the upper limit for runs was exactly 13. Therefore, Test 1 showed only common cause variation.

   • The longest run was a run of four (from week five through eight), whereas a run of eight is required to indicate a shift in the process. Therefore Test 2 indicated only common cause variation.

- Test 3 requires at least six points consecutively ascending or descending for a statistical trend. However, in this process the longest series of consecutively ascending or descending points is only four (weeks three through six).

- Some might observe the 40 days delay in week 14 and conclude this point is a special cause. However, it does not trip any of the tests for a special cause.

2. Because this run chart has 20 points and only common cause variation, the process is judged to be stable and predictable (median = 31 days delay). However, it is not functioning at an acceptable level.

3. The correct management approach is not to interpret the week with 40 days' wait time or the four consecutive upward points as special causes. Investigating individual data points in a common cause system as though they were special causes will not be productive and may even be counterproductive. Instead of pulling patient charts and looking for someone to blame, the CQI team should develop a plan to change the *entire process*. However, if a special cause had been present, the correct strategy would have been to investigate and eliminate it before deciding whether or not to change the process.

4. At the time the new process is implemented, the team should lock in (or "freeze") the centerline (median) of the run chart, and then collect more data. If the next eight weeks show an average waiting time of less than 31 days, this would indicate a shift in the process, a special cause as determined by Test 2 of the run chart tests. The intervention would be a success. However, if the wait times were below the median for three or four weeks and then moved back above the median, or continued moving back and forth over the median, then the intervention was either not implemented properly, or the attempted solution was ineffective.

ENDNOTE

1. F. Sweed and C. Eisenhart, "Tables for Testing Randomness of Groupings in a Sequence of Alternative," *Annals of Mathematical Statistics* 14 (1943): 66–87.

2

Control Chart
Theory Simplified

The first chapter described some basic concepts in statistical thinking with respect to process improvement: 1) the methodological differences between conducting basic research and measuring process improvement; 2) a simple process improvement plan; 3) the need to plot data in a time series, rather than merely comparing before and after measures; 4) the difference between common and special cause variation and how this difference should determine the strategy for improving a process; 5) how an easy-to-use tool, the run chart, can be used to assess the type of variation and the effectiveness of an improvement plan.

This chapter describes a more powerful tool than the run chart for analyzing variation and measuring process improvement, namely, the control chart developed by Walter Shewhart. The chapter begins by explaining the basic elements of a control chart, four tests for detecting a special cause using a control chart, and how to choose the best control chart for the type of data being collected. It concludes with one case study to illustrate these concepts and demonstrate how a control chart is used to document a successful intervention.

CONTROL CHARTS VERSUS RUN CHARTS

Both the run chart and the control chart have the same purpose: to distinguish common from special cause variation in the data produced by a process. The type of variation should guide managers both in their overall approach to improving a process and in evaluating the effectiveness of efforts to improve a process.

Note: Major portions of this chapter appeared previously in the *Journal of Ambulatory Care Management* 25, no. 2, (April 2002): 78–88, and are reprinted here with permission.

The reader will recall from the first chapter that common cause variation means that a process is *stable and predictable*, while a special cause is a signal that a process has *changed*. A *run chart* is often a good first step in assessing the type of variation. A run chart has certain qualities that make it an attractive choice over a control chart. It is simple to construct because it requires no computer hardware or software. It can be easily constructed with paper and pencil. It can also be used with any process (clinical, operational, or financial) and any type of data (measurement data, count data, percentages, or ratios). The tests for a special cause with a run chart are few and simple to interpret.

By comparison, a *control chart* is a more sensitive and more powerful tool than a run chart.[1] The control chart has a centerline, as does a run chart. But, in addition, it also has *control limits*. Control limits provide additional tests to identify special cause variation and therefore enable managers to detect some special causes that a run chart will miss. They will also enable managers to estimate the *capability*[2] of a stable process, that is, to more accurately predict the performance boundaries of a stable process.

Nevertheless, this additional sensitivity and power come at a price. Managers must assess the type of data their processes produce and choose the appropriate control chart for these data. On the other hand, instead of choosing the best chart after data have been collected, the better approach is to begin by collecting data in such a format that you can use the best chart. Finally, although control charts can be constructed with some difficulty using paper and pencil, efficient use of control charts will require the use of a computer.

BASIC ELEMENTS

Figure 2.1 provides an example of the basic elements of a control chart. The sample data describe the delay measured in days between reading abnormal mammograms and obtaining biopsies to confirm the diagnoses. Notice that a control chart is similar to a run chart in several ways. First, similar to a run chart, the control chart is a running record of behavior over time. In this example, "weeks" is the unit of time across the horizontal (or "X") axis. Second, the quantitative measure of the characteristic being measured is listed on the vertical (or "Y") axis. In this case, it is the "average days delay per week." Third, both control charts and run charts have centerlines. However, the centerline of a run chart is the *median*, whereas the centerline of a control chart is the *mean*, or arithmetic average, of all subgroups (in this instance, all weeks).

The added sensitivity and power of the control chart comes from the addition of upper and lower *control limits*, which are marked on the chart as "UCL" and "LCL." If no special causes are present, a manager can estimate the future capability of a process from the mean and upper and lower control limits. The control limits also allow for additional tests for a special cause over and above those described for a run chart in the previous chapter.

The upper and lower control *limits of a process are not to be confused with the upper and lower* confidence *limits of a distribution.* Control limits describe the variability of a *process*, while confidence limits describe the variability of a *distribution* of data.

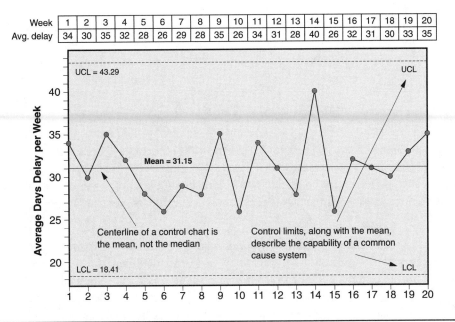

Week	1	2	3	4	5	6	7	8	9	10	11	12	13	14	15	16	17	18	19	20
Avg. delay	34	30	35	32	28	26	29	28	35	26	34	31	28	40	26	32	31	30	33	35

Figure 2.1 Basic elements of a control chart.
Weekly average of delays between an abnormal mammogram and biopsy.

A control chart examines data in a *time-series* design. If a point falls outside a control limit, this point is called a *special cause*. It is a signal that the process is not stable. Comparison charts look at data grouped in a *distribution* without respect to the order in which they were gathered. If a point falls outside a confidence limit, it is referred to as an *outlier*. This means that one can judge within a specified level of confidence (for example, 95 percent or 99 percent) that the outlier is different than the mean (average) of that distribution.

Control charts and comparison charts are complementary to each other; each offers decision makers a different view of data. Control charts show whether a process is stable so that valid comparisons can be made. Comparison charts tell a provider how their performance compares with others in its comparison group. However, *comparison charts have no statistical validity unless the process is in control. When a process is in control*, comparison charts can tell an organization whether they should continue to monitor a process so as to maintain its current level of performance or whether it should try to improve its current level of performance. Lee and McGreevey (2002a) provide an excellent explanation of the difference between control and comparison charts in describing how the Joint Commission uses these charts in accreditation surveys.[3]

Finally, those who construct their own control charts, rather than use a software program, should keep in mind that the standard deviation (or *sigma*) of a *control chart* is not computed in the same way as the standard deviation of a *distribution*. In fact, the control limits for each type of control chart are computed with different formulae.

Managers need not commit these formulae to memory. However, they do have to know how to choose the appropriate chart for the data at hand and then allow the computer software to compute the correct mean and control limits.

DETECTING SPECIAL CAUSES

Many rules have been offered to detect the presence of a special cause in control charts. However, for the purposes of simplicity, only four tests are discussed in this chapter. They will usually be adequate for most healthcare processes and will maintain a middle road between missing special causes that are present and finding spurious special causes.

Test #1: A special cause is indicated when a single point falls outside a control limit.
The only test for a special cause that Shewhart employed was the presence of one or more points beyond the UCL or LCL. It is important to note that Shewhart set both control limits at three standard deviations (or sigmas), not two. This was a pragmatic decision. He felt the three-sigma test was the best tradeoff between making two opposite mistakes or errors: either deciding a special cause was present when there was none (Type-I error), or deciding that no special cause was present when one was actually present (Type-II error). Both types of error have negative consequences, but cannot be completely eliminated. *If the data are normally distributed*, the probability of having a single point outside either three-sigma control limit *by chance when the process has not changed* is rare, approximately three in a thousand. However, the exact probabilities will change depending on the shape of the distribution of the data. Those who are tempted to use two-sigma limits *as a standard decision rule* should read Wheeler's explanation of Shewhart's rationale for using three sigmas.[4] Grant and Leavenworth (1988) also support the standard use of three sigmas and explain how the probability of Type-I error varies with the shape of the distribution.[5]

Test #2: A special cause is indicated when two out of three successive values are: a) on the same side of the centerline, and b) more than two standard deviations from the centerline. Although Shewhart only used Test #1, he did allow for judgment to be used in developing additional detection rules. Test #2 was first published in the Western Electric Company's *Statistical Quality Control Handbook* (1984). It is a logical extension of Test #1. Because it involves the use of more than one point, it is considered to be a "run-test." It is useful in detecting a change in a process that is smaller in size than that detected by Test #1. Since this test requires the addition of a two-sigma line for an exact determination, it is usually not the first choice after Test #1. However, it is often possible to make a visual judgment as to whether two out of three values are more than two standard deviations from the centerline even without the two-sigma line. (See Figure 2.2.) If added, the two-sigma lines would appear two-thirds of the distance away from the centerline toward both control limits.[6]

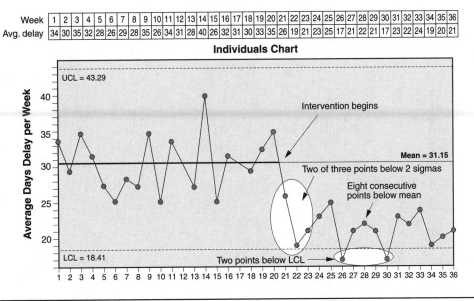

Week	1	2	3	4	5	6	7	8	9	10	11	12	13	14	15	16	17	18	19	20	21	22	23	24	25	26	27	28	29	30	31	32	33	34	35	36
Avg. delay	34	30	35	32	28	26	29	28	35	26	34	31	28	40	26	32	31	30	33	35	26	19	21	23	25	17	21	22	21	17	23	22	24	19	20	21

Figure 2.2   Weekly average of delays between an abnormal mammogram and biopsy.
Three tests for a special cause document the success of the intervention; mean and control limits are based on the first 20 weeks before intervention.

Test #3: A special cause is indicated when eight or more successive values fall on the same side of the centerline. This test was also published in the Western Electric Handbook as another additional run-test for a special cause. Because of its simplicity, Test #3 is often the first choice for a test to use along with Test #1. This test will detect a smaller, but consistent shift in a process that both Tests #1 and #2 might miss. This test is the same as that used with the run chart, although the centerline of a run chart is the median. Test #3 is demonstrated in Figure 2.2, where a run of 16 consecutive points falls below the baseline mean of 31.15 days.

Test #4: A special cause is indicated by a trend of six or more values in a row steadily increasing or decreasing. A trend is also included as an "unnatural pattern" in the Western Electric Handbook, but no numerical value for length is given. Most authors generally require a minimum of six values without a change in direction for a "trend" with less than 20 data points, or seven in a row when there are 20 or more points. Trends will be rare in healthcare data, but the test is useful to restrain those who are quick to interpret a series of three or four points moving in the same direction as a special cause. This test is also the same as that used with a run chart.

Figure 2.2 demonstrates the additional power in detecting a special cause that a control chart provides over a run chart. In this control chart, the mean and control limits were based on the first 20 weeks and then were "locked in" when an improvement effort was introduced. The reason for locking in the mean and control limits is that a process with at least 20 data points and no evidence of a special cause is *stable*. This means that,

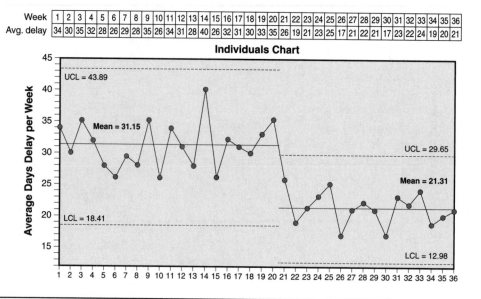

Week	1	2	3	4	5	6	7	8	9	10	11	12	13	14	15	16	17	18	19	20	21	22	23	24	25	26	27	28	29	30	31	32	33	34	35	36
Avg. delay	34	30	35	32	28	26	29	28	35	26	34	31	28	40	26	32	31	30	33	35	26	19	21	23	25	17	21	22	21	17	23	22	24	19	20	21

Figure 2.3   Historical chart showing process capability before and after an intervention.
Intervention was implemented after week 20. The special cause has become a new common cause system.

if nothing further is done to change the process, then one can predict that the process would continue to average about 31.15 days delay, although any individual week might find the average as high as 43 days delay or as low as 18 days delay.

Was the intervention that was introduced after week 20 successful in reducing the delays? The answer is a resounding "yes" because one can see several signs of special cause variation. Two of the first three weeks after the intervention begins (weeks 21–23) are beyond two sigmas from the mean (Test #2). The values in weeks 26 and 30 are beyond the LCL (Test #1). There are also eight or more successive values on the same side of the centerline during weeks 21 to 36 (Test #3). Using the run chart tests, it would have taken eight weeks before one could detect a special cause, while the control chart detected the special cause within three weeks time.

Figure 2.3 shows how the data in Figure 2.2 might be reformatted to show that the special cause has now become a new common cause system. The former process averaged 31 days delay. The new process after the successful intervention has an average of about 21 days and appears to be stable. A control chart divided into two or more time periods in this fashion is sometimes referred to as a "historical chart." It can be useful in presentations to boards of trustees (see chapter 8).

Should the Tests for a Special Cause Ever Be Modified?

These tests were originally developed for manufacturing processes where the primary concern was often avoiding "false alarms" that would result in shutting down an assembly process. They are recommended as standard practice. However, in health-care there may be occasions where the rules should be modified. The decision is based on whether the greater concern is missing a special cause or in wasting time and energy investigating too many "false" special causes. For example, three-sigma limits may be acceptable when dealing with late food trays or the number of days it takes to mail patient invoices. On the other hand, physicians might feel that when patient lives are involved, they should not wait until a data point exceeds three sigmas before taking action. When the well-being of patients is at risk, a case can be made for using two-sigma limits as "early warning limits," or for using six rather than eight points with Test #3.

HOW MANY SUBGROUPS ARE REQUIRED FOR A CONTROL CHART?

A control chart should have about 20 to 25 data subgroups to apply the four tests described above. With fewer than 20 subgroups, there is increased danger of missing special causes (Type-II error). However, if you observe a special cause with less than 20 subgroups, investigate it. With more than 30 subgroups there is increasing danger of finding special causes due to chance (Type-I error). Some would argue for modifying the tests to allow for this increased probability. Once again, I recommend the use of the four tests described above as standard practice.

CHOOSING THE APPROPRIATE CONTROL CHART

Identifying the Type of Data

The choice of the appropriate control chart begins with identifying the type of data being collected. As was mentioned earlier, there is only one kind of run chart, and it can be used with any type of data. However, there are many different kinds of control charts, and the appropriate choice will be determined by the type of data being collected.

Figure 2.4 shows that the choice of a control chart begins with deciding on the type of data at hand. There are two basic types of data:

1. *Measurement* data (often called "continuous" or "variable" data)

2. *Count* data (often called "discrete" or "attribute" data)

Measurement data can take on different values on a *continuous scale*. Measurement data can have as many decimal places as a measuring instrument can read (for example, waiting time in minutes, time to do something, body weight in grams, length of stay in days, and so on). Sometimes whole numbers can be treated as measurement data (for example, the total number of procedures performed, total number of drugs administered, total revenue or expenses, and so on, in a given time period).

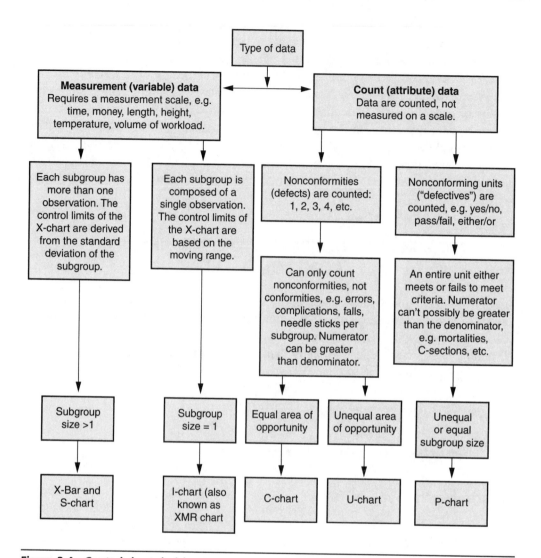

Figure 2.4   Control chart decision tree.

Count data, as the name suggests, are counted, and not measured on a scale. However, the counts can be of two kinds:

1. Nonconforming *units* of some kind

2. *Nonconformities*

However, *in both types of count data, only whole numbers are counted.* There is no continuous scale.

A *nonconforming unit* means that an entire unit either meets, or fails to meet, some criterion. These data are dichotomous, or binomial—either/or, yes/no, pass/fail—type of data. For example, a patient is discharged either alive or dead; a delivery was either a C-section or a vaginal birth; a patient either fell or did not fall during a hospital stay.

In the manufacturing arena, this type of count data is often referred to as "defective" units. In these instances, the numerator (for example, number of patients who fell) is a subset of the denominator (for example, the total number of patients discharged).

Another approach to count data is to count not just nonconforming units, but all *nonconformities*—or all "defects." For example, instead of merely recording that a patient fell during a hospital stay (a nonconforming unit), one could count *all of the times* a patient fell (nonconformities). With this approach the numerator (for example, number of falls) is not a subset of the denominator and can theoretically be greater than the denominator (for example, number of patient days).

Deciding on the Best Chart

After determining the type of data that have been collected, the next step is to consult the control chart decision tree (Figure 2.4). The reader should be aware that there are many other types of control charts not noted on this chart, including the NP-chart, X-Bar and R-chart, and an exponentially weighted chart. Figure 2.4 represents an effort to simplify the choices by presenting only five control charts. These five charts should be adequate for most situations in healthcare.[7]

P-chart. The P-chart ("P" stands for either "percent" or "proportion") is the most easily understood and perhaps most often used control chart. It is the chart of choice when the data collected are count data of nonconforming *units*, for example, mortalities or C-sections. The "subgroup" will be the unit of time across the horizontal axis, which might be "month," while the percent of mortalities or C-sections would be plotted on the vertical axis. The denominator will almost always be different each month, but plotting the "percent," rather than the absolute number of nonconforming units, will adjust for this difference in "area of opportunity." The case study at the end of this chapter illustrates the use of a P-chart.

U-chart. The U-chart (let "U" stand for "unequal area of opportunity") is the appropriate chart for counts of *nonconformities where there is an unequal area of opportunity*. For example, if data were collected on the number of patient falls during a given week or month, it would be highly unlikely that the number of patient days would be the same from period to period. To account for this difference in the opportunity for patient falls, it would be helpful to divide the total number of falls (including multiple falls by an individual patient) by the total number of patient days in each period—thus producing a *ratio* of falls to patient days. This is a more powerful way to detect a change in the patient safety process than using a P-chart to plot the percentage of patients who fell in each time period. The learning point here is that managers should try to collect data so that they can use the *better* chart. A U-chart (or a C-chart) is generally more powerful than a P-chart.

C-chart. A C-chart is an alternative to the U-chart for counts of *nonconformities where there is an equal—or virtually equal—area of opportunity* (let "C" stand for a "constant area of opportunity"). When the denominator is virtually the same, that is, does not vary from the average by more than about 20 percent, then managers can plot the *actual count* of nonconformities (for example, the total number of falls) for each time period.[8] A concrete number is often easier for many to understand than a ratio.

In practice, a U-chart and C-chart are often used together to provide a different perspective on the process. Figure 2.5 is a U-chart that displays the ratio of "code blues" per patient day. The UCL varies with the census. Figure 2.6 is a C-chart which displays the actual number of "code blues" with the assumption that the "area of opportunity" is virtually the same from month to month. The UCL is a straight line. The process is pictured in a very similar way. Neither chart exhibits a special cause.

I-chart. Measurement data can be gathered in different ways. When each "subgroup," or data point, is composed of a *single observation*, then the appropriate chart is the I-chart, which is a brief way of saying "individual values and moving range chart." Figure 2.2 is an example of an "individuals" or I-chart.[9] (Some prefer to call the I-chart an "XMR" chart, where "X" stands for "individual value," and "MR" stands for "moving range chart." The choice of terminology is a matter of personal preference.) An I-chart has many applications. For example, it can be used to track net operating margin, total expenses, total revenue, total number of procedures, or total number of patients.[10]

X-bar and S-chart. When measurement data are collected so that each subgroup has *more than one* observation, the appropriate chart is the X-bar and S-chart. "X-bar" stands for "average" and "S" stands for "standard deviation." One example of the appropriate use of an X-bar and S-chart would be to assess whether or not the length of hospital stay for a given type of patient had changed over time. It is also commonly used to measure turnaround time, for example, with lab tests (see Figure 2.7).[11] The S (or sigma) chart examines variation *within* each day, while the X-bar (average) chart examines variation *between subgroups over time.* Neither of these charts shows a special cause.

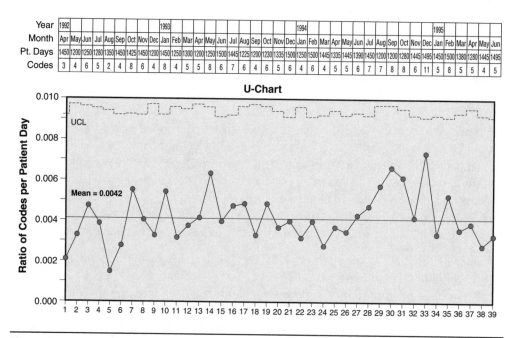

Figure 2.5   Ratio of Code Blues per patient day—all units.

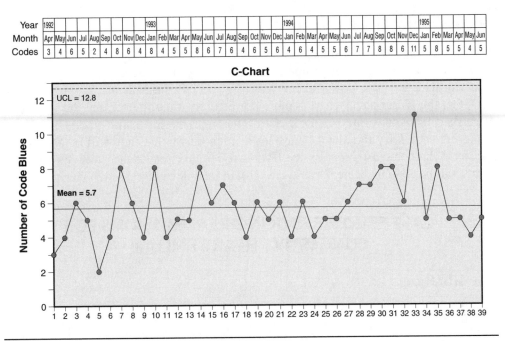

Year	1992									1993												1994													1995				
Month	Apr	May	Jun	Jul	Aug	Sep	Oct	Nov	Dec	Jan	Feb	Mar	Apr	May	Jun	Jul	Aug	Sep	Oct	Nov	Dec	Jan	Feb	Mar	Apr	May	Jun	Jul	Aug	Sep	Oct	Nov	Dec	Jan	Feb	Mar	Apr	May	Jun
Codes	3	4	6	5	2	4	8	6	4	8	4	5	5	8	6	7	6	4	6	5	6	4	6	4	5	5	6	7	7	8	8	6	11	5	8	5	5	4	5

Figure 2.6   Number of Code Blues per month—all units.

Day	1	2	3	4	5	6	7	8	9	10	11	12	13	14	15	16	17	18	19	20	21	22	23
Test 1	86	90	101	76	102	81	75	92	93	109	70	80	85	69	106	89	85	95	72	95	75	60	77
Test 2	73	82	74	71	76	82	50	65	71	92	84	79	63	71	93	95	101	89	60	84	97	110	55
Test 3	75	95	89	105	115	55	95	93	82	76	67	58	110	112	82	73	68	88	97	61	115	56	99

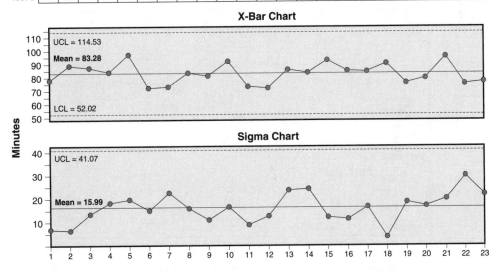

Figure 2.7   CBC turnaround time from lab to ED (X-bar and S-chart), using a sample of three tests each day for 23 consecutive weekdays.

Which Control Chart Is the Best?

The appropriate chart for a situation depends on a number of factors. My goal here is to provide an overview of possible choices. In general, it can be said that the charts for measurement data are more powerful for detecting special causes than charts for attribute data; that the X-Bar and S-chart is more powerful than the I-chart; and the C-chart or U-charts is more powerful than the P-chart. Therefore, the key learning point here is that managers should try to collect their data in such a way that they will be able to use the *better* chart, not just a *correct* one. There are certain circumstances where each of the charts will be contraindicated. These circumstances will be discussed in chapter 5.

CASE STUDY: REDUCING READMISSIONS FOR CONGESTIVE HEART FAILURE

The Situation

A large hospital system discharged about 40 to 60 patients per month with a primary diagnosis of congestive heart failure (CHF). The physicians were distressed that in some months 15 to 20 percent of those discharged were readmitted within 90 days for the same diagnosis. A case management team was organized to design and implement a better plan for discharge planning and follow-up care. Historical data were collected for 1998 and 1999. The case management protocol was implemented in January 2000 and followed for the next 12 months. Figure 2.8 displays the data from January 1998 to December 2000.

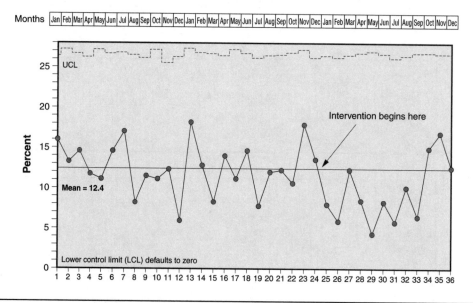

Figure 2.8   Percent CHF readmissions: 1998 to 2000.
The 1998–1999 mean (12.4%) is locked in at the time of the intervention. UCL is "stair-stepped" because the number of monthly discharges varies.

Questions

1. Why did the team choose a P-chart?

2. Was the plan effective?

3. What further questions need to be addressed?

Analysis and Interpretation

1. The team chose a P-chart because the number of patients readmitted each month is considered count data of "nonconforming units" or of "defectives." That is, the data were binomial data: each patient was either readmitted within 90 days, or not. The data were subgrouped by month. Notice that the UCL is uneven, or "stair-stepped," because the number of discharges each month varies. The LCL defaults to zero, because the exact LCL is less than zero, and it is not possible to have a negative percentage.

2. The plan was definitely successful, at least for a while. During the 24 months from January 1998 to December 1999, the data showed a stable system with only common cause variation and a mean of 12.4 percent readmissions per month. Therefore, the team locked in the mean at the time the case management team implemented the new patient care protocol in January 2000. The percent of readmissions for the first nine months of 2000 was below the centerline, a special cause (Test #3).

3. During the last three months of 2000, the percentage of readmissions moved back above the centerline. The team has to inquire about the reason for this. Were the data collected accurately? Was the operational definition of "readmission" changed? Did some physicians stop using the new protocol?

ENDNOTES

1. Some experts find the expression "control" chart to have a negative connotation and prefer the name "Shewhart" chart after its developer, Walter Shewhart. I like the idea. However, I will continue to use the terminology "control chart" throughout this book with the hope of avoiding confusion.

2. The word *capability* to some statisticians means the ability to meet some specifications. I use it here as a general description as to how well a process is performing.

3. K. Lee and C. McGreevey, "Using Control Charts to Assess Performance Measurement Data," *Journal on Quality Improvement* 28, no. 2 (February 2002a): 90–101.

4. D. J. Wheeler, *Advanced Topics in Statistical Process Control* (Knoxville, TN: SPC Press, 1995): 345–250.

5. E. L. Grant and R. S. Leavenworth, *Statistical Quality Control* (New York: McGraw-Hill, 1988): 65–66.

6. In our book published in 2001, Dr. Lloyd and I followed the common practice of dividing the area between the mean and the upper and lower control limits into "zones." We also used an additional test for a special cause used in Western Electric's *Statistical Quality Control Handbook* (1984), four or five consecutive points in Zone B (that is, beyond one sigma). In recent years I have found that this test leads to too many spurious special causes.

7. The readers who are familiar with the book, *Measuring Quality Improvement in Healthcare: A Guide to Statistical Process Control Applications* (Carey and Lloyd 2001), will notice that the current article uses a slightly different decision tree in choosing an appropriate control chart. While either approach may be followed in practice, the approach used in this article is an effort to simplify the selection process.

8. The exact percentage of variance that one is willing to accept is arbitrary. I prefer 20 percent. But it is not uncommon to see a number chosen between 15 percent to 25 percent.

9. Some prefer the terminology "XMR" chart to "I-chart," where "X" stands for "individual value," and "mR" stands for "moving range chart." The choice of terminology is a matter of preference. Notice that the moving range chart is not shown in Figure 2.2. The reason for its omission will be explained in chapter 4.

10. Some would use the I-chart exclusively for all control charts. The problem with this approach will be discussed in chapter 5.

11. The control limits of the X-bar (or average) chart of the X-bar and S-chart are derived from the standard deviation of each subgroup, whereas the control limits of the X-chart of XMR chart are computed from the moving range. Those familiar with my earlier book (Carey and Lloyd 2001) will also notice that I have dropped the X-bar and R-chart and now recommend the X-bar and S-chart with subgroups greater than one. I will explain the reason for this in chapter 4.

Part II

Advanced SPC Theory and Methods

3

Drilling Down into Aggregated Data

THE CHALLENGE

Let us suppose that you have chosen a set of indicators to measure your performance on selected financial, administrative, and clinical processes. You summarize the results with aggregate statistics and list them quarterly on a dashboard or balanced scorecard. Now the difficult question: How do you go about improving the results?

For example, let's examine a partial list of measures for an eight-hospital system as they are displayed on a scorecard in Table 3.1.

As we discussed in chapter 1, demonstrating process improvement by comparing two aggregated measures—before and after an intervention—can be misleading. To truly understand how well a process is performing, and whether or not the aggregated data are meaningful, it is necessary to begin by looking at data in a time-series design and then examining the type of variation. In chapter 2 we described how a control chart is used to distinguish common and special cause variation. We also discussed how the type of variation would guide managers in their approach to improving the process:

- Did they find special cause variation? Then the correct approach is to conduct root cause analysis. If the cause is negative, eliminate it. If positive, make the cause a part of the future process.

- Did they find common cause variation? Then decide whether or not the process is functioning at an acceptable level. If not, then change the process.

In either case we need a theory and a way to test the theory. First, let us examine the four steps in drilling down into aggregated data and then look at two case studies to see how these steps are applied.

Table 3.1   Worldbest Healthcare System balanced scorecard

Measure	Current Quarter	Last Quarter	Goal
CABG mortality	2.8%	2.7%	Less than 2%
C-section rate	21%	20%	Less than 19%
Intubation time for CABG surgery	7.5 hours	7.6 hours	Less than 6.5 hours
Cycle time for lab tests to ED	59 minutes	60 minutes	Less than 40 min.
Patient satisfaction with physician care	80% Maximum achievable score (MAS)	78% MAS	80% MAS

STEP 1. CREATE THE APPROPRIATE CONTROL CHART AT THE AGGREGATE LEVEL

Response to Special Cause Variation

If a control chart displaying the aggregate data for your entire organization (hospital system, hospital, health plan, long-term care facility, and so on) reveals a special cause, you need to ask why the data underlying the special cause are different from the common cause data:

- Do you have accurate data? Was there an error in data entry?

- Did the operational definition change?

- Did the method for collecting or reporting the data change?

- Did any outside event (for example, a Joint Commission survey, a change in organizational structure, change in reimbursement, and so on) influence the process?

- Was there a change in personnel or method of delivery?

- Can you use a Pareto chart or a histogram to analyze the data?

After you have identified the special cause, remove it (if it is a negative special cause), incorporate it (if it is a positive special cause), and then re-create the chart. Is the process at the aggregate level now *stable and acceptable* as measured by your target? If so, lock in the current mean and control limits and continue to monitor the process. If it is not acceptable, then move to Step 2.

Response to Common Cause Variation

- Is the process functioning at an acceptable level, that is, is it meeting the current target or goal? Then lock in the current mean and control limits and continue to monitor it.

- If the process is not meeting current expectations (target or goal), then you may want to improve it. However, improving a common cause system often presents a greater challenge than improving an unstable one. You can't just give people a pep talk and tell them to "work harder!" If working harder is all that is necessary, you can wonder why they didn't work harder last year. You need to develop a theory as to where the problem lies and then a plan to address the problem. You are ready to move on to Step 2.

STEP 2. STRATIFY ALL ORGANIZATIONAL UNITS ON THE SAME CONTROL CHART

Do you feel that the aggregate data may hide variation among your organizational units? Then the next step is to display the data for all the units on the same control chart to determine whether any unit is a special cause when viewed as part of the entire system. For example, if you are looking at aggregate data for your hospital, do you feel that there might be variation between nursing units or between departments? Then display the data for those units or departments on the same chart using rational ordering or rational subgrouping.

Rational Ordering

Rational ordering means that the data for all units are presented *sequentially* using *time-ordered data* (for example, weeks, months, quarters, and so on) in such a manner that you have enough data points for a solid chart, that is, approximately 20 points. For example, if you are disaggregating data for a five-hospital system, you might plot four quarters of data from Hospital A, followed by the same four quarters from Hospital B, and so on.

Rational Subgrouping

Rational subgrouping means that instead of arranging the data sequentially in a time series, you would aggregate all the data for each unit and do a *cross-sectional comparison* of the various organizational units you selected, using *only one data point for each organizational* unit. When using rational subgrouping, the *data points are no longer connected* because you are not looking at the data over time.

Rational subgrouping is a good alternative to rational ordering either when there is very little data for each unit, or there are so many units that a control chart using rational ordering would become too cluttered. An example of rational subgrouping of hospitals will be seen in Figure 5.5 of chapter 5, where four hospitals are compared on the basis of heart surgery mortality. Figure 3.5 in the first case study in this chapter is an example of rational subgrouping of individual obstetricians on the basis of their C-section rates. Each point represents the rate for an individual physician based on all his/her deliveries for the entire year. Because of the large number of physicians being compared, it would be impossible to plot 12 months of data for each physician on the same chart.

Rational subgrouping is most commonly done using a P-chart for attribute data, or an X-bar and S-chart for variable data. (You cannot use rational *subgrouping* with I-charts because by definition each point on an I-chart represents a *single* observation.)

Respond Appropriately to the Observed Variation

After stratifying all units on the same chart using either method, did you find that one or more units were a *special cause*? Now you need to answer more questions. Is the special cause unit(s) stable? If not, why did the special cause occur inside this unit? If the unit is stable, why is one unit a special cause when compared to the other units? Creating a separate control chart for each unit will help address these questions. (Go to Step 3.)

Did you find only *common cause* variation after stratifying the organizational units? Then you will want to look at other process variables and stratify the data using rational ordering or rational subgrouping. (Go to Step 4.)

STEP 3. CREATE A SEPARATE CONTROL CHART FOR EACH ORGANIZATIONAL UNIT

If one unit is a special cause when viewed in relationship to the other units, you then have to ask whether each unit's process is stable when viewed by itself. To answer this question, you would develop a *separate time-ordered control chart* for each unit, using time periods that will give you approximately 20 subgroups. For example, you might plot the last 20 months of data for each unit. If you found a *special* cause, then you would proceed to investigate the root cause and eliminate it as you did in Step 1 with aggregated data.

If the unit that was a special cause when viewed in relationship to the other units is *in itself* a stable but unacceptable system, then you would develop a theory as to how you would change this process. You would use the plan–do–study–act cycle (explained in chapter 1) to implement changes and evaluate the effectiveness of interventions. After implementing the change, you would hope to see a *positive* special cause—a sign that your improvement plan worked.

STEP 4. STRATIFY ON OTHER PROCESS VARIABLES

Now let us suppose that when you stratified the data by organizational unit (Step 2), you continued to see only common cause variation. Then you might want to disaggregate your data based on a different theory. For example, do you think that perhaps the aggregated data are covering over differences among providers, DRGs, treatment modalities, severity status, days of the week, shifts, and so on? For example, do you theorize that mortality rates for heart surgery might differ significantly among surgeons, that C-section rates might differ significantly among obstetricians, or that lab cycle time to the ED differs by day of the week or by shift? Then proceed to stratify the data on the appropriate control chart based on your theory using rational ordering or rational subgrouping.

If you find a special cause, then proceed to conduct root cause analysis as in Step 1. Did you find a stable, but unacceptable, process? Then use the plan–do–study–act cycle to implement changes and evaluate the effectiveness of the interventions.

The four steps in the drill-down process described above are diagrammed in Figure 3.1 and are illustrated in the two case studies that follow.

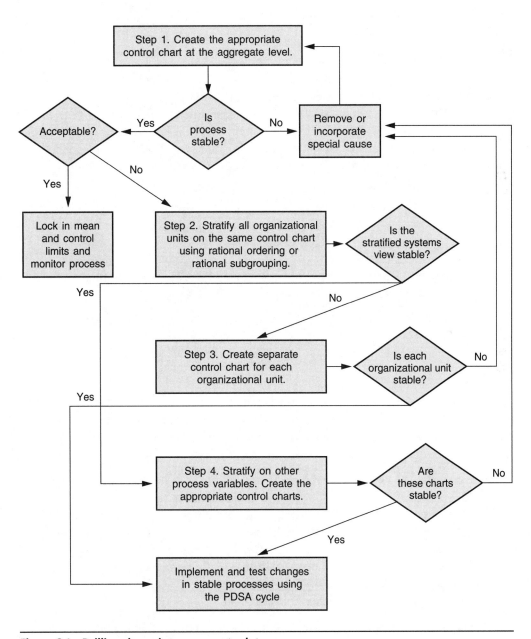

Figure 3.1   Drilling down into aggregate data.

CASE STUDY: REDUCING C-SECTION RATES

Key Learning Points

1. Drilling down into aggregated data to improve a process

2. The steps to improve a process with common cause variation

3. Using rational ordering and rational subgrouping

The Situation

The largest purchaser of care of the Worldbest Healthcare System complained that the average C-section rate at Worldbest had increased from 1999 to 2000 and was now over 21 percent. The average at other area hospitals was between 17 percent and 19 percent. The purchaser told Worldbest that it expected them to lower the C-section rate to below 19 percent if they wished to remain on their provider list. Worldbest responded by making a P-chart on the combined monthly C-section rate for all eight hospitals in the system (Figure 3.2).

Questions

1. Why did they make a P-chart?

2. Did Figure 3.2 show any special causes? Had the C-section rate increased over the last year?

3. What should Worldbest do next if it wished to reduce the C-section rate in its system?

Analysis

1. Worldbest made a P-chart because the number of C-sections is count (attribute) data. It used the last 24 months of data because it is desirable to have at least 20 data points to be reasonably certain of detecting special causes.

2. Figure 3.2 shows that the average C-section rate over the last two years was 20.2 percent. There were no special causes. The first seven months of 1999 were below the mean (20.2 percent), but a run of eight would be required for a special cause. Therefore, it would be correct to say that the process had not changed over the last two years. Nevertheless, the provider was requiring that the average be less than 19 percent. With over 20 points and common cause variation, Worldbest could predict that the next year would continue to average 20.2 percent unless some changes were made.

3. The next step would be for Worldbest to stratify all its eight hospitals on the same chart, using rational ordering of the data. (See Figure 3.3.)

Month	Jan	Feb	Mar	Apr	May	Jun	Jul	Aug	Sep	Oct	Nov	Dec	Jan	Feb	Mar	Apr	May	Jun	Jul	Aug	Sep	Oct	Nov	Dec
Year	1999												2000											
Deliveries	1483	1436	1601	1595	1724	1614	1715	1707	1623	1590	1409	1491	1482	1407	1626	1569	1649	1552	1638	1487	1563	1606	1442	1479
All CS	286	285	316	305	336	311	343	353	298	330	294	298	308	303	339	324	333	326	343	291	298	349	299	306
Percent	19.3	19.8	19.7	19.1	19.5	19.3	20.0	20.7	18.4	20.8	20.9	20.0	20.8	21.5	20.8	20.7	20.2	21.0	20.9	19.6	19.1	21.7	20.7	20.7

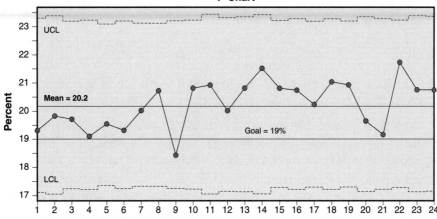

Figure 3.2   Total C-sections aggregated from all eight hospitals: 1999–2000.

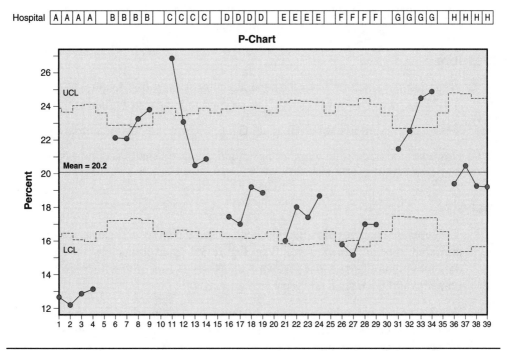

Figure 3.3   Rational ordering of C-sections for eight hospitals using six-month periods: 1/99–12/00.

Questions

4. Why did Worldbest use semiannual data to rationally order its eight hospitals on the same chart (Figure 3.3)?

5. What did they learn from Figure 3.3?

6. What step should be taken next?

Analysis

4. Worldbest used semiannual data because it wanted to have at least 20 points on its chart, but not so many that the chart would be too cluttered to analyze.

5. Worldbest learned that five of its eight hospitals were special causes, that is, their processes were different from the system as a whole. Two hospitals (A and F) were *positive* special causes, and three (B, C, and G) were *negative* special causes! Four hospitals (A, D, E, and F) were already performing C-sections at or below the 19 percent goal. Hospital H, while not a special cause, appeared to be performing C-sections at about a 20 percent rate.

6. First, Worldbest has to investigate the reasons for the special causes. Then, it would make *separate control charts for each hospital*, using *monthly* data for 1999 and 2000 so as to have the 20 or more points required for a solid P-chart. However, for the purpose of this case study, we will look at a separate chart only for Hospital G (Figure 3.4), which had one of the highest overall rates and also appeared to have an "upward trend" on Figure 3.3.

Questions

7. What do you conclude from the separate control chart for Hospital G (Figure 3.4)? Was there an "upward trend" as seemed to appear in Figure 3.3?

8. What can you predict about Hospital G's C-section rate for the coming year?

9. How can you determine whether or not a decrease in the C-section rate will really be beneficial?

Analysis

7. The separate chart for Hospital G does not show any special cause. What appeared to be an "upward trend" on Figure 3.3 (four points of semi-annual data moving upward) is not a trend. At least six consecutively increasing points would have been necessary for a trend.

8. With 24 points and common cause variation, we can predict the C-section rate for Hospital G will be about 23.4 percent for the coming year—unless some change is made in the process.

9. At this point, it might be worthwhile to see whether the purchaser of care was correct in asking that the C-section rate be reduced. To answer this question,

one might construct a *scattergram* (Figure 3.5), comparing C-section rates with "negative outcomes" as defined by the obstetricians. For example, "negative outcomes" might be operationally defined as uterine ruptures, third or fourth degree lacerations, infections, neonatal mortality, and so on.

Month	Jan	Feb	Mar	Apr	May	Jun	Jul	Aug	Sep	Oct	Nov	Dec	Jan	Feb	Mar	Apr	May	Jun	Jul	Aug	Sep	Oct	Nov	Dec
Year	1999												2000											
Deliveries	340	335	368	335	412	350	383	400	335	316	329	324	321	300	351	361	381	333	357	351	334	347	311	303
C-Section	75	73	89	59	92	77	88	90	80	65	78	69	82	81	80	100	77	87	92	75	82	89	72	87
Percent	22.1	21.8	24.2	17.6	22.3	22.0	23.0	22.5	23.9	20.6	23.7	21.3	25.5	27.0	22.8	27.7	20.2	26.1	25.8	21.4	24.6	25.6	23.2	28.7

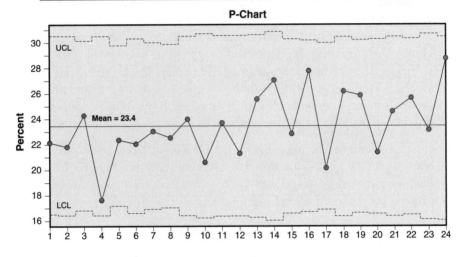

Figure 3.4   Hospital G—total C-sections for 1999–2000.

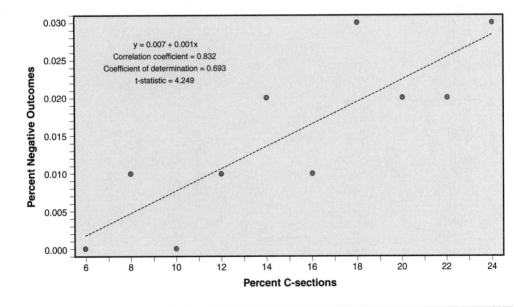

Figure 3.5   Relationship between C-section rate and "negative outcomes."

Questions

10. What do you learn from Figure 3.5?

11. What should be done next at Hospital G?

Analysis and Interpretation

10. Based on these (hypothetical) data there is a positive linear relationship (correlation coefficient = 0.83) between the percent of "negative outcomes"— as operationally defined by the obstetricians at this hospital—and the C-section rate. Therefore, it would appear that there would be some merit in trying to reduce the C-section rate as requested by the purchaser of care. However, this relationship would not be the same at every hospital, especially if "negative outcomes" were defined differently. There might well be a point at which the C-section rate might become so *low* that we would observe an *increase* in negative outcomes, such as neonatal hypoxia. A scattergram would provide an insight into this question based on each hospital's own experience.

11. Hospital G might also ask whether there was a difference in C-section rates between the 19 physicians who delivered babies at Hospital G. To answer this latter question, they would stratify the physicians on a control chart using rational subgrouping. (See Figure 3.6.)

MD ID#	13	23	20	7	16	8	19	3	10	21	22	2	1	4	18	12	15	6	9
Deliveries	324	333	334	335	335	340	347	350	351	351	357	383	400	412	614	621	645	721	742
C-Sections	69	77	82	73	80	75	89	77	60	75	102	88	90	92	147	193	143	148	187
Percent	21.3	23.1	24.6	21.8	23.9	22.1	25.6	22.0	17.1	21.4	28.6	23.0	22.5	22.3	23.9	31.1	22.2	20.5	25.2

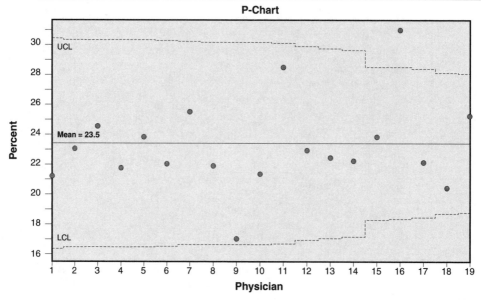

Figure 3.6   Stratifying C-section rate by physician at Hospital G: 1999–2000.

Questions

12. What can you learn from Figure 3.6? What can you conclude about physician #12?

13. Why aren't the data points connected?

14. How might Hospital G proceed in its effort to reduce its C-section rate?

Analysis and Interpretation

12. There is one special cause, namely, physician #12. This physician's rate (31.1 percent) is far above the UCL. One must not conclude that his rate is "too high" without first investigating his practice. In fact, in this instance, a high percentage was justified because physician #12 was the most experienced at Hospital G and other physicians often sent their high-risk cases to him. On the other hand, physician #10 (17.1 percent) and physician #22 (28.6 percent) seemed to be quite different from the other physicians. However, in fact their rates do not differ from the overall rate of 23.5 percent at Hospital G. Neither physician is a special cause in relation to the current practice at Hospital G.

13. The data points aren't connected because this control chart is using rational subgrouping to compare physicians. We are not looking at whether the process is improving over time. This practice might be referred to as using a control chart for *cross-sectional comparisons.*

14. Hospital G should now use its 1999–2000 data (Figure 3.4) as a baseline from which to measure the effect of changes it will introduce to reduce the C-section rate. Because it has 24 points showing a stable process, it will lock in (or "freeze") the centerline of the chart at 23.4 percent. If the data during the coming year show a special cause, this would be a signal that the "improvement plan" worked. To develop an improvement plan, the physicians at Hospital G might confer with the physicians at Hospital A to see why their C-section rate was so much lower than at the other seven hospitals in the system. Did their deliveries have the same level of risk? Did they hire a full-time OB specialist to be on-call at all times to advise staff obstetricians on when it would be advisable to do a C-section ? Did they institute the practice of giving monthly feedback to individual obstetricians on their C-section rates? They could introduce one change at a time, using the plan–do–study–act cycle.

Question

15. Let us suppose that Hospital G's first improvement effort was to provide monthly reports to all obstetricians on their C-section rates for the previous month. The first reports began with the month of January 2001. Figure 3.7 is a chart of the C-section rates for the years 1999 to 2001. The mean is based on the baseline data from 1999–2000. Was the intervention effective?

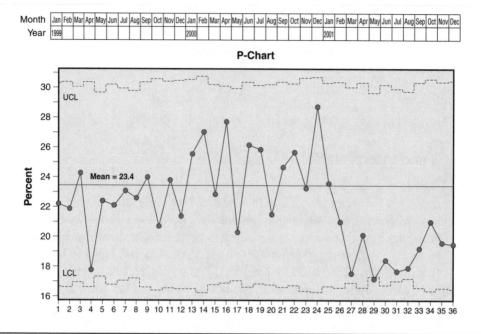

Figure 3.7   Hospital G: C-section rate before and after intervention in January 2001.
Centerline (23.4%) is extended from 1999–2000. Special cause (11 points below centerline) is a signal of a successful intervention.

Analysis and Interpretation

15. A run of 11 consecutive points below the centerline beginning in February 2001 is a special cause—a shift in the process—and a signal that the intervention was effective. Additional special causes (a point beyond the LCL and two of three consecutive points near the LCL) emphasize the degree of success. Therefore, the data from February to December 2001 now form a new common cause system. Figure 3.8 shows that Hospital G's new process capability of 18.8 percent for 2001 meets the purchaser's requirement of having an average of less than 19 percent C-sections.

CASE STUDY: CYCLE TIMES FOR LABORATORY ANALYSIS IN THE EMERGENCY DEPARTMENT[1]

Key Learning Points

1. Drilling down in aggregate data to improve a process

2. The use of an I-chart with rational ordering

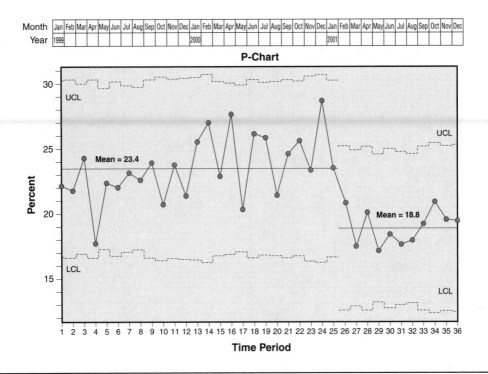

| Month | Jan | Feb | Mar | Apr | May | Jun | Jul | Aug | Sep | Oct | Nov | Dec | Jan | Feb | Mar | Apr | May | Jun | Jul | Aug | Sep | Oct | Nov | Dec | Jan | Feb | Mar | Apr | May | Jun | Jul | Aug | Sep | Oct | Nov | Dec |
| Year | 1999 | | | | | | | | | | | | 2000 | | | | | | | | | | | | 2001 | | | | | | | | | | | |

Figure 3.8   Hospital G: process capability before and after invervention in January 2001.
The new process average (18.8 percent) meets the purchaser's requirement of "less than 19 percent."

3. Subgrouping strategies

4. The importance of maintaining time order when subgrouping

The Situation

A hospital chartered an improvement team to work on reducing the long waits in the Emergency Department (ED). Recent measures had identified turnaround time (TAT) on routine blood and urine analysis as a source of delays. Complaints alleged that the average TAT was an hour, and sometimes delays were even longer. The team wanted to investigate the source of the delays and to look for ways to reduce TAT.

First, the team operationally defined TAT as the number of minutes between collection of the sample (as recorded on the container) and the time that the laboratory results were available in the ED computer system. One of the physicians on the team asked her assistant to download TATs for the tests she had requested during the last week. Table 3.2 shows the TAT for 42 routine tests along with additional information about the conditions under which each test was handled: the lab that handled the test (A, B, or C), the ED shift on which the request was made (first, second, or third), and the type of test (blood tests labeled as "X" or urine tests labeled as "Y").

Table 3.2   Lab turnaround time data with each factor identified.

Test	Lab	Shift	Type	Time	Day	Test	Lab	Shift	Type	Time	Day
1	A	1	X	60	Mon	22	A	1	Y	61	Thur
2	B	1	Y	70	Mon	23	B	2	X	58	Thur
3	C	2	X	48	Mon	24	C	2	Y	57	Thur
4	A	2	Y	58	Mon	25	A	3	X	60	Thur
5	B	2	X	68	Mon	26	B	3	Y	61	Fri
6	C	3	Y	52	Mon	27	C	3	X	58	Fri
7	A	3	X	60	Mon	28	A	1	Y	65	Fri
8	B	1	Y	71	Tues	29	B	3	X	58	Fri
9	C	1	X	.46	Tues	30	C	2	Y	61	Fri
10	A	2	Y	67	Tues	31	A	2	X	55	Fri
11	B	2	X	65	Tues	32	B	2	Y	57	Sat
12	C	3	Y	52	Tues	33	C	3	X	57	Sat
13	A	3	X	55	Tues	34	A	1	Y	64	Sat
14	B	2	Y	63	Wed	35	B	1	X	56	Sat
15	C	3	X	52	Wed	36	C	1	Y	63	Sat
16	A	1	Y	55	Wed	37	A	1	X	54	Sun
17	B	1	X	64	Wed	38	B	1	Y	54	Sun
18	C	2	Y	56	Wed	39	C	2	X	67	Sun
19	A	2	X	54	Wed	40	A	2	Y	62	Sun
20	B	2	Y	63	Thur	41	B	3	X	50	Sun
21	C	3	X	53	Thur	42	C	3	Y	66	Sun

Questions

1. How should test data be analyzed and presented to the team for study?

2. What type of control chart is appropriate for these data?

Analysis and Interpretation

1. The first step was to analyze the data at the aggregate level, in a time-ordered design—using either a run or control chart—to see whether the process was stable and predictable (that is, had only common cause variation). If a special cause was evident, the team would investigate and eliminate it. If the process was stable and predictable, but unacceptable, then they would develop some theories about factors that might be causing the delays.

2. Because TAT is measurement data, the choice was between the two variable charts (X-bar and S- or I-chart). Because each test had a single measurement, the I-chart (Figure 3.9) was the proper choice (see the decision tree in Figure 2.4, page 20).

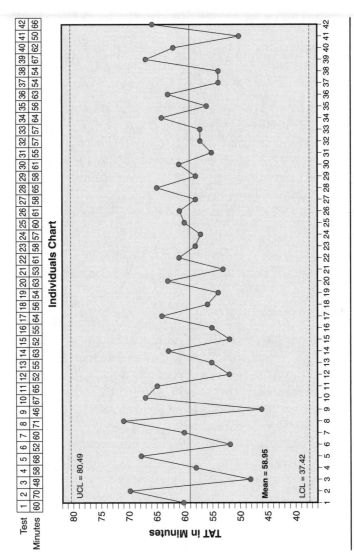

Test	1	2	3	4	5	6	7	8	9	10	11	12	13	14	15	16	17	18	19	20	21	22	23	24	25	26	27	28	29	30	31	32	33	34	35	36	37	38	39	40	41	42
Minutes	60	70	48	58	68	52	60	71	46	67	65	52	55	63	52	55	64	56	54	63	53	61	58	57	60	61	58	65	58	57	55	57	57	64	56	63	54	67	62	50	66

Individuals Chart

Figure 3.9   **Turnaround times (TAT) for routine lab tests for one week.**

Questions

3. Did Figure 3.9 show common or special cause variation?

4. What should the next step be?

Analysis and Interpretation

3. Figure 3.9 shows common cause variation. The process is stable and predictable with an average TAT of 58.95 minutes. Because the ED had set a goal of 40 minutes for the average TAT, the process was unacceptable.

4. When the chart from aggregated data shows only common cause variation, rational ordering or rational subgrouping is a powerful method of analyzing the sources of variation. Therefore, the team's next step was to identify factors that might influence TAT and to use these factors as a basis for rational ordering. Using rational ordering, the team analyzed differences between shifts (Figure 3.10), between the two types of tests (Figure 3.11), between days of the week (Figure 3.12), and between the three labs (Figure 3.13).

Question

5. Did any of these four charts reveal one or more special causes?

Analysis and Interpretation

5. The only chart that showed a special cause was Figure 3.13, which "rationally ordered" the TATs for the three labs on the same I-chart. Lab A had only common cause variation. However, both Labs B and C had special causes. Lab B had three special causes: two points above the UCL, a run of seven points above the centerline—as well as a trend of six consecutively descending points. Lab C also showed evidence of special cause variation with two points below the LCL and a run of nine points below the centerline.

Question

6. What steps should the team take next?

Analysis and Interpretation

6. First, the team would develop separate control limits for each lab (Figure 3.14). We observe that Lab A's process is stable. However, the control limits for Lab A would be considered only "trial limits" because there were only 14 data points. Next, the team would ask experts familiar with the process to investigate the reasons for the special causes in Labs B and C. Why had the TAT improved in Lab B at the same time that the TAT increased in Lab C? Could insights gained from answering these questions be helpful in also improving the TAT in Lab A?

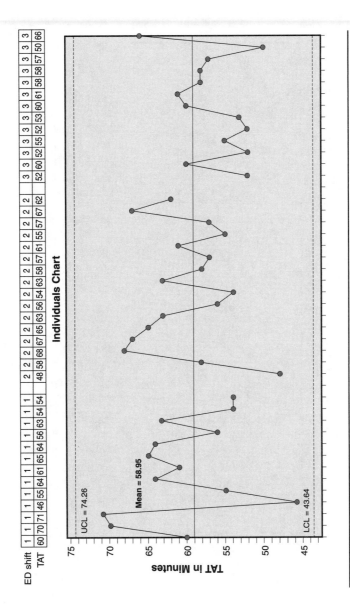

Figure 3.10 Turnaround times (TAT) by shift.

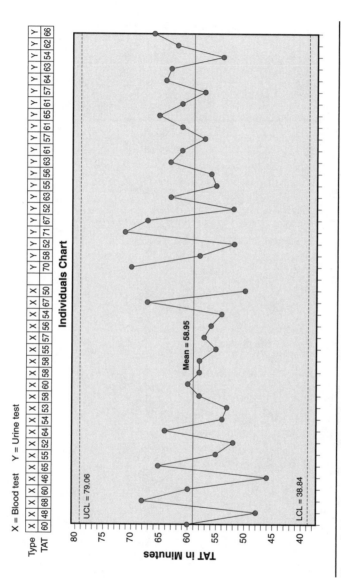

Figure 3.11 **Turnaround times (TAT) by type of test.**

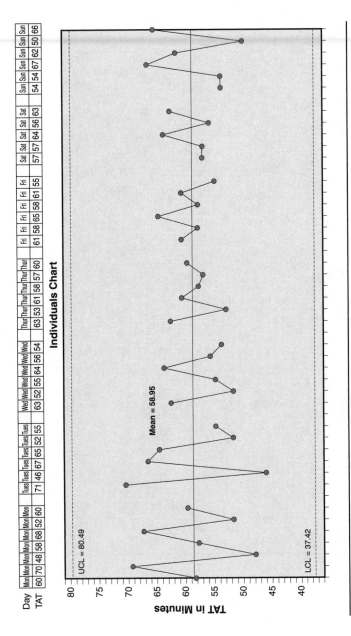

Day	Mon	Mon	Mon	Mon	Mon	Tues	Tues	Tues	Tues	Tues	Wed	Wed	Wed	Wed	Wed	Thur	Thur	Thur	Thur	Thur	Fri	Fri	Fri	Fri	Fri	Sat	Sat	Sat	Sat	Sat	Sun	Sun	Sun	Sun	Sun
TAT	60	70	48	58	68	52	60	71	46	67	65	52	55	63	52	55	64	56	54	63	53	61	58	57	60	61	58	65	58	61	55	57	64	56	63	54	54	67	62	50	66

Individuals Chart

Mean = 58.95

UCL = 80.49

LCL = 37.42

TAT in Minutes

Figure 3.12   Turnaround times (TAT) by day of week.

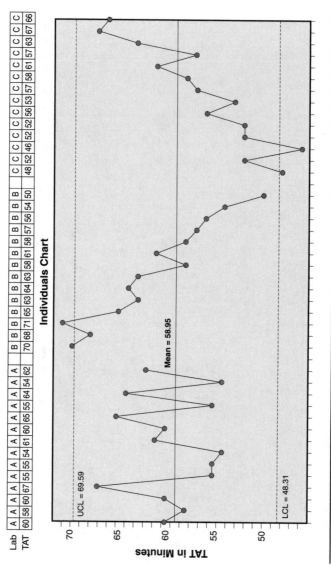

Figure 3.13   Turnaround times (TAT) rationally ordered by laboratory service.

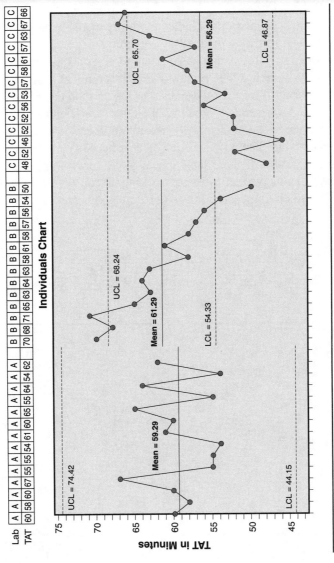

Figure 3.14 Turnaround times (TAT) with separate control limits for each lab.

The Result of the Investigation into the Special Causes

The report from Lab B revealed that one of the sample centrifuge instruments in Lab B had been down for repair earlier in the week. The repair company had loaned them two smaller centrifuge instruments that could be used until theirs were repaired. The two smaller instruments allowed them to start their test procedure more quickly for samples since they had to wait only one-half as long to fill the instrument with sample tubes. The team decided to initiate a discussion with the laboratory manager about using the appropriate type of centrifuge instruments in all of the three laboratories.

The negative drift in Lab C was due to a temporary staffing issue. Lab C already had some smaller instruments that required less batching of samples. These small instruments were purchased for the other labs. Data were then collected for 25 samples after the new centrifuges were integrated into the three labs (Figure 3.15). Observe that the aggregated TAT process now displays only common cause variation, and is therefore stable and predictable. The process is acceptable because it meets the ED's goal of a 40-minute average TAT. All three labs appear to be functioning at about the same level. The process can now be monitored by "locking in" the new mean and control limits as a baseline by which to measure future performance.

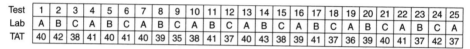

Test	1	2	3	4	5	6	7	8	9	10	11	12	13	14	15	16	17	18	19	20	21	22	23	24	25
Lab	A	B	C	A	B	C	A	B	C	A	B	C	A	B	C	A	B	C	A	B	C	A	B	C	A
TAT	40	42	38	41	40	41	40	39	35	38	41	37	40	43	38	39	41	37	36	39	40	41	37	42	37

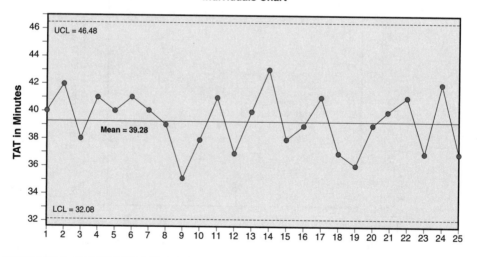

Figure 3.15   Aggregated TAT after change in laboratories.
Average TAT now meets the ED's goal of 40 minutes. TAT is now stable and predictable.

ENDNOTE

1. This case study is not based on actual lab data, but is intended to illustrate the drill-down approach described in this chapter. The author wishes to express his gratitude to Lloyd Provost for his assistance in developing this case study.

4

Issues with Control Charts

In this chapter I want to address issues that have frequently been raised during my seminars on the use of control charts in healthcare, especially by those who have been using control charts for some time. Because SPC is an art, as well as a science, some of these issues or questions do not have a "right" or "wrong" answer. Therefore, it is not surprising that experts in SPC may disagree regarding these issues. My intention is not to resolve theoretical differences, but to suggest approaches that I have found to be practical and useful in healthcare situations.

DETERMINING THE NUMBER OF SUBGROUPS

Grant and Leavenworth succinctly articulated the underlying rationale for addressing this issue: "The determination of the minimum number of subgroups required before control limits are calculated is a compromise between a desire to obtain the guidance given by averages and control limits as soon as possible after the start of collecting data and a desire that the guidance be as reliable as possible. The fewer the subgroups used, the sooner the information thus obtained will provide a basis for action, but the less the assurance that this basis for action is sound."[1]

As a general working rule, in order to use the four tests for a special cause we presented in chapter 2, authors generally agree that it is best to have 20 to 30 subgroups. When you have less than 20 subgroups, you run the danger of Type-II error, namely, missing a special cause. After you have 25 subgroups, the increased power provided by additional subgroups is minimal. When you have more than 35 to 40 subgroups, you run a higher risk of Type-I error, namely, finding a spurious special cause.

Technically speaking, you could have a control chart with only two subgroups. Referring to X-bar and R-charts or X-bar and S-charts, Shewhart wrote: "It appears reasonable, therefore, that the criterion [control limits] may be used even when we have only two subsamples of size not less than four."[2] However, Shewhart used only the "a point beyond three-sigma" test for a special cause.

Trial Limits

When you have less than 20 subgroups, some authors will refer to the control limits generated as "trial limits." By this term they are suggesting that you should be aware that you may have insufficient power to detect a special cause. If you find a special cause with less than 20 subgroups, it is worth your time to investigate. However, with less than 20 subgroups you should be hesitant to predict the future of the process and should continue to recompute the mean and control limits as more data become available. Once you have 20 subgroups and only common cause variation, then you may judge with some degree of confidence that a process is stable and predictable.

THE CAPABILITY OF A PROCESS

Why do you need to know the capability of a process? For two reasons. First, there is no way to know whether a process needs to be improved unless its present capability is known. Even though a process is stable, stability doesn't tell us whether the process is functioning at an acceptable level. Second, if an improvement plan is developed to improve a process, there is no way to determine whether the plan resulted in an improvement unless the process capability is known before and after the change.

There are different approaches to analyzing process capability.

Histograms

A frequency distribution is a good initial step toward estimating process capability. For example, if you are looking at turnaround time of lab tests, you can use a histogram to picture the shortest, longest, and modal times. However, a histogram describes the past, but does not predict future performance.

Capability Ratios

Industry often uses capability ratios, such as C_p or C_{pk}. These ratios describe the ability of a process to meet specification limits. For this reason, they are not ordinarily useful for healthcare because we do not set specification limits for most of our processes. For example, it is difficult to set specification limits for the number of mortalities, C-sections, medication errors, and so on. However, as we learn more about the use of control charts for monitoring individual patient care, there may be instances where we can speak of specification limits. For example, there are specification limits (INR range) for the use of Warfarin in anticoagulation therapy. We may also be able to set specification limits for some operational measures, for example, turnaround time for lab tests. As Wheeler points out: "None of the numerical summaries of capability should be interpreted without reference to a histogram of the individual values plotted against the specification limits. Likewise, none of the numerical summaries of capability are meaningful in the absence of a reasonable degree of statistical control (which can only be ascertained by a control chart)."[3]

Probability Plots

Some authors, such as Hart and Hart (2002) favor probability plots to estimate process capability.[4] Probability plots have the advantage of providing reasonable results for moderately small samples, which histograms will not do. However, as Montgomery rightly points out: "Histograms and probability plots summarize the performance of the process. They do not necessarily display the *potential* capability of the process because they do not address the issue of *statistical control*. . . . The control chart should be regarded as the primary technique of process-capability analysis."[5]

Control Charts

I agree with Montgomery that using a control chart is the best method to estimate process capability. How do we do this? First, gather sufficient data for a minimum of 20 subgroups. Second, ascertain whether the process is stable and predictable, that is, has only common cause variation. If special causes are present, one cannot estimate process capability with any degree of confidence. If you observe only common cause variation, then use the mean and upper and lower control limits to describe process capability. The control limits then serve as "performance boundaries."

A problem may arise in the event that you have "stair-stepped" limits, as you would with most P-charts or U-charts. If you observe a great deal of variation in the limits in these charts due to large differences between subgroup sizes, then use *only the mean* to describe process capability. The reason for this is that the control limits will change as the subgroup size changes. However, to avoid using stair-step limits, it is not an uncommon practice to set some rule of thumb for the *degree of difference from the average subgroup size* you are willing to accept, say 20 percent. Then, using the standard P-chart formula, compute straight-line limits based on the *average* subgroup size. This means that you only have to do a *single* computation when calculating the limits by hand. (The better software programs, for example, CHARTrunner2000, will easily handle this option.) For example, look back at Figure 3.4 in chapter 3 (page 37). Observe that the UCL and LCL for C-sections at Hospital G are stair-stepped limits. However, if I had set a 20 percent difference from the average subgroup size as acceptable, then Figure 3.4 could be computed with straight-line limits, as you observe in Figure 4.1. I can now be comfortable in estimating process capability using the mean (23.4 percent), the UCL (30.3 percent) and LCL (16.6 percent). This means that, if nothing changes in this process, I can predict that the C-section rate for the coming year will average

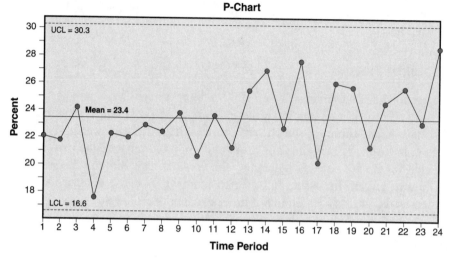

Month	Jan	Feb	Mar	Apr	May	Jun	Jul	Aug	Sep	Oct	Nov	Dec	Jan	Feb	Mar	Apr	May	Jun	Jul	Aug	Sep	Oct	Nov	Dec
Year	1999												2000											
Deliveries	340	335	368	335	412	350	383	400	335	316	329	324	321	300	351	361	381	333	357	351	334	347	311	303
C-Section	75	73	89	59	92	77	88	90	80	65	78	69	82	81	80	100	77	87	92	75	82	89	72	87
Percent	22.1	21.8	24.2	17.6	22.3	22.0	23.0	22.5	23.9	20.6	23.7	21.3	25.5	27.0	22.8	27.7	20.2	26.1	25.8	21.4	24.6	25.6	23.2	28.7

Figure 4.1   Hospital G—total C-sections for 1999–2000.
Straight-line limits were developed using a 20 percent tolerance for subgroup size.

about 23.4 percent, although in any given month the rate might go as high as 30.3 percent or as low as 16.6 percent.

GRAPHICAL GUIDELINES FOR CONSTRUCTING CONTROL CHARTS

Control charts should be constructed so as to provide others with sufficient details to evaluate the accuracy and appropriateness of your chart, but not so much detail as to distract them from the main story that the chart is telling. The following are some choices you need to make.

Displaying the Raw Data

It is usually a good practice to provide others with the raw data used to construct the control chart. This is preferably done on the chart itself (as was done in Figure 4.1), but the data might also have been made available on a separate table. This practice enables the reader to have confidence in the chart. For example, the readers of Figure 4.1 would know that each subgroup had sufficient data for a solid P-chart. In chapter 5 we will discuss problems caused by insufficient data. If a special cause had appeared on this chart, the reader would also be able to more easily check on the possibility of data entry errors.

On the other hand, it is advisable not to present the raw data on the chart itself if the chart would become so cluttered that presenting all the data would detract from the main message. This is sometimes the case when the number of subgroups is over 30. For example, Figure 4.2 is a reproduction of Figure 3.2 from chapter 3. In this figure the main message was to show the extraordinary amount of variation between the eight hospitals in the system, and the advisability of constructing separate control charts for each of the eight hospitals. Semiannual subgroups accomplished this purpose without the need of presenting raw data. (Also notice that because of the special causes, it would not be appropriate to estimate the capability of the process.)

Chart Titles

Each chart should be titled in such a way that the focus of the chart as well as the difference between this chart and other charts being presented is clear. The key message that the chart is meant to convey might be described in a subtitle. It is usually a good idea to also note the type of control chart that was constructed (for example, a P-chart, U-chart, and so on) somewhere on the page, unless you are presenting an entire series of the same type of charts, for example, to a board of trustees. (See how these three suggestions are illustrated in Figure 4.1.)

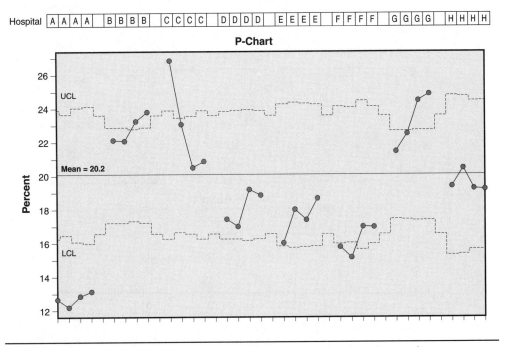

Figure 4.2 Rational ordering of C-sections for eight hospitals using six-month periods: 1/99 to 12/00.

I-Charts

A difference of opinion arises with respect to the presentation of the I-chart (also called an "individuals" or an "XMR" chart). The full name of the I-chart is an "individual values and moving range chart." As we will see in a case study later on in this chapter, the I-chart is a "paired chart," that is, there is an average chart (the X-chart) and also a moving range (MR) chart from which the control limits of the average (X) chart are computed. Most experts would suggest as general practice to display only the average (X) chart so as not to distract the reader from the main message of the X-chart. As Wheeler points out: "The ultimate argument in favor of the mR (sic) chart is not that it improves the ability of the X-chart to detect signals, but that it serves as a reminder of the correct way of computing limits for the X-chart."[6] My own opinion is that you should not display the MR chart, although you should check the MR chart to see whether it has any points above the UCL.

For example, Figure 2.1 in chapter 2 used an I-chart to demonstrate the basic essentials of a control chart. In Figure 2.1 the MR chart was not displayed. Now look at the same chart with the MR displayed (Figure 4.3). The entire story is conveyed by the average (X) chart (which this software program refers to as an "individuals" chart). Because there are 20 subgroups with only common cause variation, the capability of the process can be estimated. If nothing changes, one can predict that during the coming weeks the average delay will be about 31 days, although in any given week the average delay might be a long as 43 days or as short as 18 days. The MR chart has no

Week	1	2	3	4	5	6	7	8	9	10	11	12	13	14	15	16	17	18	19	20
Avg. delay	34	30	35	32	28	26	29	28	35	26	34	31	28	40	26	32	31	30	33	35

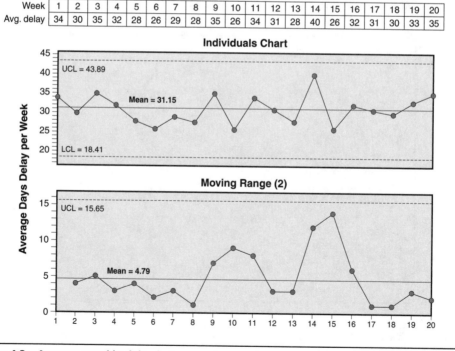

Figure 4.3   Average weekly delay between abnormal mammogram and definitive biopsy.

special cause (that is, no point above the UCL). Therefore, we can conclude that the limits of the average chart were calculated correctly. In this case, the presentation of the MR chart only distracts from the main story being communicated by the X-chart.

However, while the main message is usually clear from the X-chart, there are occasions when the moving range chart can provide useful information. Therefore, it should be examined before deciding to omit it from the presentation. For example, if the MR chart is out of control, one should recompute the limits of the X-chart after removing the out-of-control points. (However, to determine special causes in the MR chart, use only Test 1 for a special cause, namely, one or more points above the UCL. The failure to recompute the limits may result in missing a special cause in the X-chart.)[7]

Finally, plotting the MR chart is also useful when there has been an *interruption* in the stream of data. In this case, the value of the moving range *across the interruption* should *not* be calculated. Many software programs ignore this issue and do not compute the interrupted I-chart correctly. For more on this point, see Hart and Hart.[8]

Zones versus No Zones

Another issue in control chart construction is whether or not to display the "zones." The zones are formed by adding one- and two-sigma lines in addition to the UCL and LCL. These lines are often added when one is using all the Western Electric Tests for a special cause, including the test: four out of five consecutive points in Zone B (between one and two sigmas) or beyond. It is difficult to use that test without displaying the one- and two-sigma lines to delineate the zones. I customarily used zones in generating the charts in my previous book (Carey and Lloyd 2001). However, in recent years I dropped the test, four out of five consecutive points in Zone B or beyond, because I was finding too many false special causes. By omitting the one- and two-sigma lines it was possible to construct a cleaner and less confusing chart and still use the test: two out of three consecutive points in Zone A (between two and three sigmas). For example, examine Figures 4.4 and 4.5. Omitting the zones makes for a clean chart and does not detract from the interpretation.

USING THE X-BAR AND S-CHART IN PLACE OF THE X-BAR AND R-CHART

In my previous book (Carey and Lloyd 2001) I advised using the average and range (X-bar and R) chart with subgroups of less than 10 measurements, and the X-bar and S-chart for subgroups of more than 10. I made this recommendation because a subgroup *range* is easier to calculate by hand than a *standard deviation*. With larger subgroups the standard deviation provides a better estimate of subgroup dispersion. With subgroups under 10, there is little difference. Now that excellent and inexpensive software programs are available, I recommend that the X-bar and R-charts be dropped, and that the X-bar and S-chart be used with any subgroup larger than one. This recommendation is meant to simplify chart selection.

Day	1	2	3	4	5	6	7	8	9	10	11	12	13	14	15	16	17	18	19	20	21	22	23
Test 1	86	90	101	76	102	81	75	92	93	109	70	80	85	69	106	89	85	95	72	95	75	60	77
Test 2	73	82	74	71	76	82	50	65	71	92	84	79	63	71	93	95	101	89	60	84	97	110	55
Test 3	75	95	89	105	115	55	95	93	82	76	67	58	110	112	82	73	68	88	97	61	115	56	99

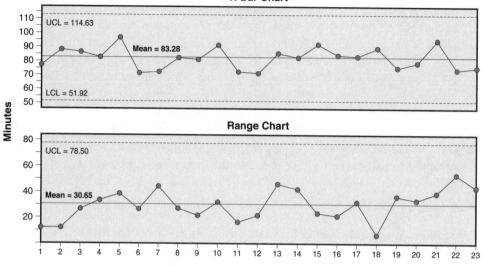

Figure 4.4   CBC turnaround time from lab to ED (X-bar and R-chart), using a sample of three tests per day for 23 consecutive weekdays.

Figures 4.4 and 4.5 demonstrate how the results are virtually identical for both the X-bar and S-charts and X-bar and R-charts with small samples. Observe that the mean in both charts is identical (83.28 minutes), while the UCL and LCL of each X-bar chart differ by less than one-tenth of a minute. The interpretation of both charts is exactly the same. Both charts show a stable, predictable process with only common cause variation.

About the X-Bar and S-Chart

The X-bar and S-chart is a paired control chart. The X-bar chart tracks subgroup averages. The S-chart tracks the standard deviations of the subgroups. Since the average standard deviation (S-bar) is used to calculate the control limits of both the X-bar and S-charts, it is best to interpret the S-chart first. When the S-chart is in control, the X-bar chart will be more believable.

When an X-bar and S-chart is used with *time-ordered* data, the subgroups are usually composed of small homogeneous samples. (See Figure 4.5.) The recommended sample size is usually four to seven. (A sample size of three was used in this example for the purpose of simplification.) These samples, often referred to as *judgment* or *rational* samples, should be as *homogeneous* as possible because one wants

Day	1	2	3	4	5	6	7	8	9	10	11	12	13	14	15	16	17	18	19	20	21	22	23
Test 1	86	90	101	76	102	81	75	92	93	109	70	80	85	69	106	89	85	95	72	95	75	60	77
Test 2	73	82	74	71	76	82	50	65	71	92	84	79	63	71	93	95	101	89	60	84	97	110	55
Test 3	75	95	89	105	115	55	95	93	82	76	67	58	110	112	82	73	68	88	97	61	115	56	99

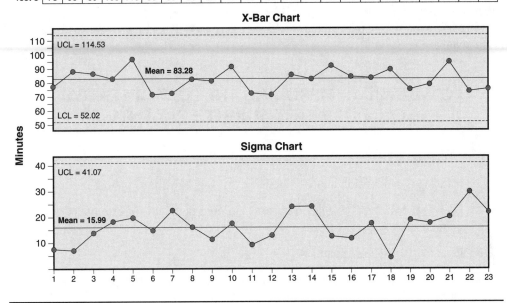

Figure 4.5   CBC turnaround time from lab to ED (X-bar and S-chart), using a sample of three tests each day for 23 consecutive weekdays.

to sample across *noise*, so that the X-chart will be better able to detect a *signal* if the process is changing.

Average charts look for differences *between* subgroups, while sigma charts look for differences *within* subgroups. Therefore, samples should be chosen in such a manner that if special causes are present, the chance for differences *between* subgroups will be maximized, while the chance for differences due to these special causes *within* a subgroup will be minimized.

The reader should be aware that rational sampling is quite different from *stratified random sampling,* which is used, for example, in patient surveys or in market research. Stratified random sampling is designed to minimize bias so that we can generalize the findings from a small sample to an entire population. In rational sampling we have an unknown amount of bias in any single sample and are not attempting to generalize to an entire population.

The X-bar and S-chart can be used not only with time-ordered data, but also to compare *rational subgroups in cross-sectional comparisons*, for example, to compare different shifts, DRGs, physicians, hospitals, or hospital units. Once again, the purpose is to make the subgroups as homogeneous as possible because we are looking for differences between subgroups. When X-bar and S-charts are used to compare rational subgroups, it is desirable to use a subgroup size of at least 20—and to keep the sample itself in time-order. A time-ordered sample of at least 20 will provide a reasonable estimate of each rational subgroup, while also allowing one to check on the stability of each subgroup. The subject of sampling will be revisited in chapter 6.

The following case study illustrates a number of the ideas I have presented thus far in this chapter.

CASE STUDY: IMPROVING THE POST-OPERATIVE CARE OF HEART SURGERY PATIENTS

Key Learning Points

1. Improving a common cause system by drilling down into the data

2. Using an X-bar and S-chart with time-ordered data and for cross-sectional comparisons

3. Estimating process capability

4. Locking in the mean and control limits to evaluate the effect of an intervention

The Situation (Step 1)

The Chair of Anesthesiology felt it might be beneficial to shorten the length of intubation (LOI) time for coronary artery bypass graft surgery (CABG) patients. Shortening the LOI would reduce the risk of infection to patients and at the same time reduce cost by decreasing ventilator time and expedite "fast-tracking" of patients.

From January 1 to December 15, 1998, 332 patients were considered noncomplicated cases in which the LOI ranged from zero hours (when a patient was extubated in the operating room) to 24 hours. There were an additional 40 surgical cases that had various complications where the LOI appropriately ranged from 40 to 310 hours. The Chair decided that the focus of the improvement effort (decreasing ventilator time) should be on the 332 noncomplicated cases.

The Chair prepared an X-bar and S-chart showing the average LOI for bimonthly periods in 1998 (Figure 4.6) and presented it at the departmental meeting for discussion.

Questions

1. Why did the Chair choose an X-bar and S-chart rather than an individuals chart (I-Chart) to analyze the data for 332 patients?

2. Why use bimonthly rather than monthly data?

3. What conclusions can you draw from this chart?

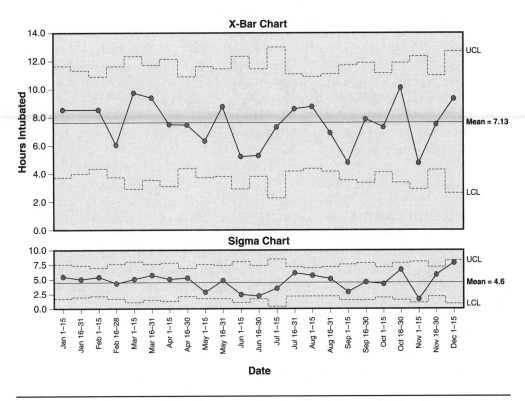

Figure 4.6   LOI for noncomplicated CABG patients—1998 (X-bar and S-chart).

Analysis and Interpretation

1. LOI is measurement (or variable) data. The purpose was to ascertain whether the process had changed over the past year. Since there are enough data to produce an effective X-bar–S-chart, this chart would be preferable to an I-chart. The reason for the preference is that the X-bar–S-chart would have narrower control limits than an I-chart using the same data and therefore be more powerful in detecting special causes. The control limits are narrower because the control limits are based on averages, rather than on individual values. Finally, an I-chart with 332 data points would be overwhelming.

2. Whenever possible, it is desirable to have 20 or more subgroups in order to estimate process capability. Monthly data would only provide 12 subgroups. However, a minimum of two cases per subgroup is required for an X-bar–S-chart. The number of surgeries each week ranged from one to 12. Therefore, the Chair chose to use bimonthly data as a compromise between weekly and monthly subgroups. Dividing the available data (from January 1 to December 15) into bimonthly time periods, 23 data points were generated for 1998.

3. Figure 4.6 shows no special causes. There are no data points outside the control limits. Although there are two "trends" of five (the first descending and another ascending), seven in a row would be required for a "trend" that is a special cause. Therefore, the anesthesiologists concluded that the LOI for 1998 was a stable and predictable process that could be expected to average 7.13 hours if nothing were done to change it. Because of the great variability in the number of cases from period to period, the control limits are stair-stepped and difficult to estimate with precision.

The Situation (Step 2)

The Chair theorized that there might be a difference in the practice patterns of the six anesthesiologists, although they were treating the same type of patients. To examine this possibility he constructed an X-Bar and S-chart to analyze the differences among anesthesiologists using six rational subgroups comprised of aggregated annual data for each anesthesiologist. (See Figure 4.7.) After examining the results from Figure 4.7, the Chair generated an I-chart to analyze Dr. Sing's LOI times (Figure 4.8).

Questions

4. What did the Chair conclude from Figure 4.7?

5. Why did the Chair subsequently construct an I-chart (Figure 4.8) with Dr. Sing's data?

6. What can you conclude from Dr. Sing's chart?

Analysis and Interpretation

4. Figure 4.7 shows that Dr. Sing was a special cause in relation to the other anesthesiologists. His average LOI is below the LCL. No other anesthesiologist is a special cause.

5. At this point it would be useful and desirable to construct separate control charts for each anesthesiologist to see whether their individual processes were stable and therefore comparable. However, we will focus on Dr. Sing because of the special cause noted in Figure 4.7.

6. An I-chart using subgroups composed of Dr. Sing's individual patients (Figure 4.8) shows that fully 25 percent of all his patients were extubated in the OR (indicated by zero hours intubation time). Separate control charts for the other anesthesiologists (not shown) revealed that *none* of them were extubating patients in the OR. The patients extubated in the OR were judged to belong to a different process and needed to be removed from the data. At the same time Dr. Sing had five patients with extubation times above the UCL. These four cases are special causes and required investigation. Because Dr. Sing's process is not stable, it is inappropriate to compare him to the other anesthesiologists.

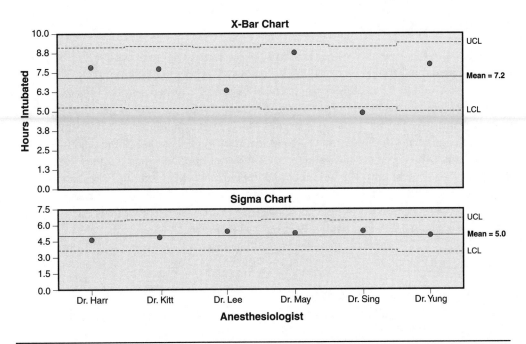

Figure 4.7   LOI for noncomplicated CABG patients by anesthesiologist (X-bar–S-chart).

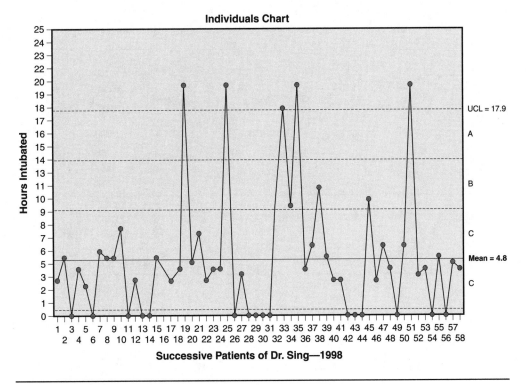

Figure 4.8   Dr. Sing—LOI for noncomplicated cases (I-chart).

The Situation (Step 3)

When the anesthesiologists reviewed the above charts at their departmental meeting, they discussed the differences in their practices with respect to extubation. Dr. Sing convinced his associates that some patients could be safely extubated in the OR, as long as the resident physicians were properly trained to reintubate patients in the intensive care unit, if necessary. Dr. Sing also discovered that his five patients with long intubation times were surgeries that took place late in the afternoon. This led to the discovery that the residents, who cared for the patients after the attending anesthesiologists left for the day, preferred to wait until the next day and consult with the attending anesthesiologist rather than extubate patients on their own initiative. As a result of the meeting, new guidelines were developed aimed at shortening LOI. These guidelines were implemented in January 1999 and data collection was resumed.

Question

7. Four months after implementing the new guidelines, another X-bar and S-chart was constructed to examine their effectiveness in shortening LOI (Figure 4.9). Were they effective?

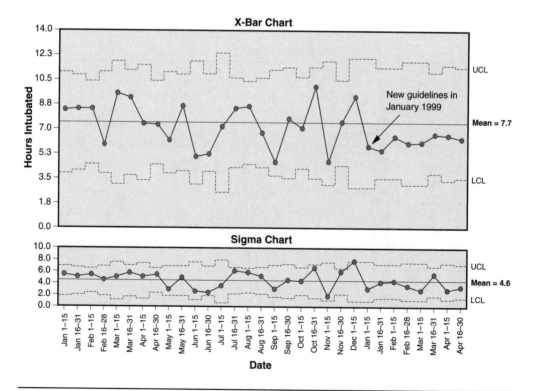

Figure 4.9   LOI before and after new guidelines (X-bar–S-chart).

Analysis and Interpretation

7. Figure 4.9 shows that the new guidelines were indeed effective. The average LOI for 1998 (after removing patients who were extubated in the OR) was 7.4 hours. The recomputed 1998 average was extended (locked in) at the time the new guidelines were introduced in January 1999. The first eight bimonthly time periods in 1999 were added to the 1998 data. A run of eight consecutive points below the mean signals a special cause and demonstrates that the process had changed.

Management Considerations

The anesthesiologists might wish to monitor the new process to see whether the improvement holds up. To do this they could construct a chart that divides the data into two periods: 1998 and 1999 (Figure 4.10). This chart shows that the new process is currently averaging 6.3 hours and seems to be stable. However, until we have at least 20 bimonthly subgroups in 1999, one must consider 6.3 hours as a "trial" mean and continue to recompute the 1999 mean and control limits as new data become available. Any additional changes in the guidelines should also be noted on the chart so their effect can be assessed.

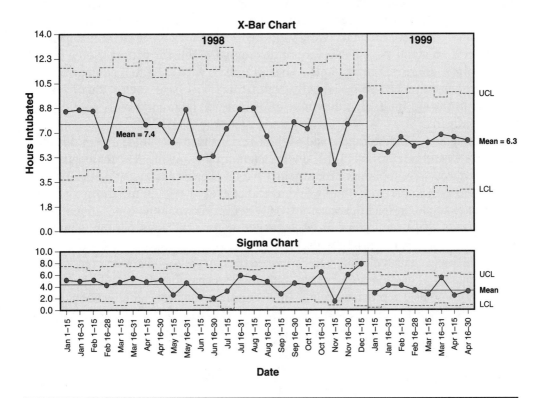

Figure 4.10   LOI before and after intervention in January 1999.

AUTOCORRELATED DATA

There is one other issue that I wish to address before concluding this chapter. A basic assumption in the standard use of control charts is that the observations are uncorrelated, that is, independent of one another. However, when data are collected successively over time, it is possible that sequential subgroups may affect one another. The term to describe this phenomenon is *autocorrelation*. Examples in healthcare data include data regarding census, accounts receivable, and delinquent patient charts. For example, the hospital census on Saturday will include patients who were there on Friday, Thursday, and possibly even earlier. If we are tracking accounts receivable, the total amount in a given month will have some overlap with the previous months. The same is true when tracking delinquent patient charts.

Two questions arise in this regard:

1. In what way does autocorrelation affect the interpretation of control charts?

2. How should the problem of autocorrelation be addressed?

First, the presence of autocorrelation can have a serious impact on the performance of control charts because it tends to increase the number of Type-I errors. In other words, there will be more spurious special causes, more "false alarms." Most common will be special causes from three-sigma violations and "trends." However, the problem becomes more serious when the "Western Electric" runs tests are used (see chapter 2).

There is no single acceptable way of dealing with autocorrelation. Some would say to simply ignore it. For example, Wheeler (1995) writes: "Small autocorrelation (even though they may be statistically significant) will have such a small impact upon the estimated limits that they may effectively be ignored in most applications of control charts."[9]

Other authors would disagree and suggest various measures to deal with this phenomenon. One way is to avoid the autocorrelation by sampling less frequently. For example, if you were looking to see whether the number of delinquent medical charts was decreasing, sample every third week instead of every week. Or use a different indicator. For example, instead of measuring daily census, it would be better to use either the number of daily admissions or discharges to track whether or not the number of inpatients we serve is increasing or decreasing.

Others argue against plotting autocorrelated data on *control* charts and recommend that the data be plotted on a *line* chart (without any centerline or control limits). The pattern that unfolds can provide insight without applying control chart methodology. In other words, control charts are not the answer for every situation. The goal is insight into the data. If a simple line chart can provide this, so much the better.

ENDNOTES

1. E. L. Grant and R. S. Leavenworth, *Statistical Quality Control* (New York: McGraw-Hill, 1988): 122.
2. W. A. Shewhart, *Economic Control of Quality of Manufactured Product* (New York: Van Nostrand, 1931): 315.
3. D. J. Wheeler, *Advanced Topics in Statistical Process Control* (Knoxville, TN: SPC Press, 1995): 193.
4. M. K. Hart and R. F. Hart, *Statistical Process Control for Healthcare* (Pacific Grove, CA: Duxbury, 2002): 131.
5. D. C. Montgomery, *Introduction to Statistical Quality Control* (New York: John Wiley & Sons, 1991): 385.
6. Wheeler, *Advanced Topics in Statistical Process Control,* 110.
7. There are different methods to recompute the limits of the X-chart when a special cause appears in the MR chart. The easiest approach is to use the alternate formula: control limits = X-bar +/– (3.14 multiplied by the *median* of the range chart) rather than X-bar +/– (2.66 multiplied by the *mean* of the range chart).
8. M. K. Hart and R. F. Hart, *Statistical Process Control for Healthcare,* p.74.
9. Wheeler, *Advanced Topics in Statistical Process Control,* 288.

5

Limitations of Attribute Charts

In general, measurements are better than counts. As a consequence, the control charts for measurement data (X-bar and S-chart and the I-chart) are usually preferred to the charts for count data (P-, C-, and U-charts). Therefore, whenever possible, one should always choose to *measure* an activity, rather than *count events*. For example, if one were looking at improving the cycle time of lab tests to the emergency department, it would be better to measure the exact cycle time in minutes of each test, rather than count the number of times the cycle time was over the "target time" (for example, over 60 minutes). In the first instance, one could plot the measurements on an I-chart. In the second instance, one would plot the percentages on a P-chart, which would require more data than an I-chart and at the same time be less precise in assessing process improvement.

ASSUMPTION OF EQUAL PROBABILITY

When the quality characteristic must be counted and cannot be measured (for example, number of mortalities, C-sections, patient falls, and so on), then one must choose the appropriate attribute chart (P-, C-, or U-chart). However, attribute charts have some constraints and limitations. For example, attribute charts assume that each event under consideration is separate and independent of the preceding and succeeding events, and also that *each event has a constant or equal probability of occurrence*.

Some experts (for example, Grant and Leavenworth 1988)[1] acknowledge the assumption of constant probability and then proceed to ignore it, because one is seldom able to prove or disprove the assumption in real-life situations. However, one is well advised to at least question whether the population remains substantially the same from subgroup to subgroup, so that equal probability between subgroups is a reasonable assumption.

Those who are uncomfortable with Grant and Leavenworth's approach to dealing with the assumption of equal probability may choose to follow Wheeler's recommendation of using I-charts in place of all attribute charts.

Using I-Charts in Place of Attribute Charts

Wheeler (1995) insists on the need to demonstrate equal probability for each event. He recommends that *as standard procedure* the I-chart (which he calls an "XmR-chart") be used in place of attribute charts "as long as the average count per sample exceeds 1.0."[2] I have not been able to find any refereed journal article that evaluates, let alone approves of, the use of I-charts for count data. However, in my experience in healthcare I have indeed found that the interpretation of the data is sometimes the same whether I-charts or attribute charts were used for attribute data. This is especially true when the numbers in the denominators run into the hundreds and do not vary much from subgroup to subgroup. However, I have also seen instances where attribute charts found special causes that I-charts missed—and that further investigation revealed to be true special causes! This happens when the denominators are small and vary from subgroup to subgroup.

Therefore, I am not comfortable with Wheeler's *blanket* recommendation that I-charts be used for all count (attribute) data. A beginner in the use of SPC might follow this recommendation, but the more advanced evaluator should be willing to be more discriminating in the choice of a chart. In similar fashion, a golfer could conceivably play golf with a *single* golf club; let's say a three-iron. But a person who aspired to play golf with greater proficiency should arguably buy a full set of golf clubs and learn how to select the best club for each shot.

The following case study illustrates how an I-chart may sometimes miss a special cause that a P-chart can identify.

CASE STUDY: NEONATAL AUTOPSIES

The Situation

A teaching hospital, St. Christopher Hospital, needed to demonstrate that it had a high percentage of autopsies for its residency programs. St. Christopher found that the percentage of autopsies had decreased over the decade from 1990 to 1999, although there had been no official change in organizational policy with respect to autopsies, and the medical staff and patient population was substantially the same. The Quality Measurement Department presented two control charts to the Quality Improvement (QI) Committee to analyze the data. One was a P-chart that showed there had been a special cause (Figure 5.1). The year 1990 was a positive special cause, and 1997 was a negative special cause. The other chart was an I-chart that did not detect any special causes (Figure 5.2).

Year	1990	1991	1992	1993	1994	1995	1996	1997	1998	1999
Deaths	38	60	67	57	49	46	53	45	32	40
Autopsies	35	44	46	32	36	24	30	16	13	26
Percent	92.1	73.3	68.7	56.1	73.5	52.2	56.6	35.6	40.6	65.0

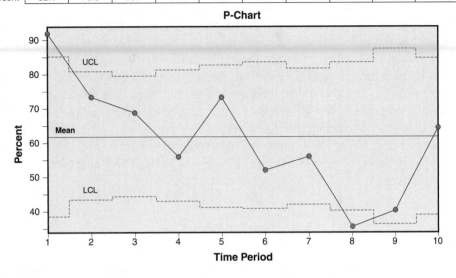

Figure 5.1   Neonatal autopsies—P-chart shows special causes.

Year	1990	1991	1992	1993	1994	1995	1996	1997	1998	1999
Percent	92	73	69	56	73	52	57	36	41	65

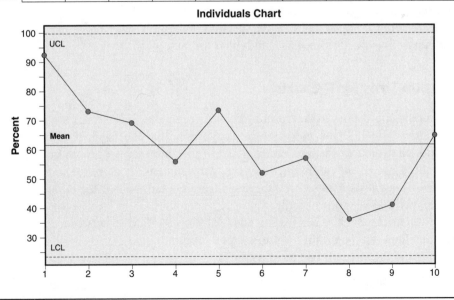

Figure 5.2   Neonatal autopsies—I-chart shows no special causes.

Analysis and Interpretation

Subsequent inquiry by the QI Committee revealed that the burden of asking the family for permission to do autopsies was assigned to the hospital chaplains. During the 1990s there was a turnover in the chaplaincy staff. The QI Committee's inquiry revealed that the new staff chaplains were not as comfortable with this responsibility and let this aspect of their ministry gradually fall by the wayside. In January 1999 a new clergyman took over as Chair of the Department of Chaplains and reminded the chaplains during their monthly staff meetings that their job description included requesting permission for an autopsy from family members following all deaths, including neonatal mortalities. As a result, the percentage of neonatal autopsies increased during 1999. The P-chart had correctly identified a special cause, which a subsequent investigation was able to correctly explain. The I-chart had missed the special cause.

SKEWNESS

Attribute charts also have a potential problem with *skewness*, that is, the centerline drifts toward zero as the subgroup size becomes smaller. If the "area of opportunity" (subgroup size) for the event under consideration is too small, then it will be difficult to determine special causes with accuracy or to detect an improvement in a process. In other words, the smaller the subgroup size, the less sensitive P-charts, C-charts, and U-charts will be to changes in the quality of the process. The problem of skewness in attribute charts is addressed by the sampling and subgrouping plan, but once again there is no general agreement on exactly how to do this. The following section presents guidelines for dealing with skewness by controlling subgroup size. The application of the guidelines is illustrated in the case study that follows.

Subgroup Sizes for P-Charts

Some simple approaches to determining the subgroup size for P-charts are presented by Montgomery (1991).[3] One guideline he suggests is that the subgroup size should be large enough to find at least one event or occurrence in every subgroup. In other words, there should not be any subgroups with a "zero percent" occurrence. Another useful guideline he suggests is to select subgroups large enough so that the control chart will have a positive lower control limit.

The American Society for Testing and Materials (ASTM) provides a couple of specific guidelines for determining the sample subgroup size for P-charts. The ASTM states that the P-chart will be "most useful":

1. When the samples are large, say when n is 50 or more and when the expected number of nonconforming units per sample is four or more, or

2. when the subgroup sample size multiplied by the average percentage (pBar)—*expressed as a proportion*—is greater than four (for example, $50 \times .08 = 4$).

The ASTM also provides two approaches for determining the *lower* limit for a subgroup size.[4] It states that a P-chart "may not yield reliable information:"

1. When subgroups have less than 25 in the denominator, or

2. when the subgroup size n multiplied by pBar is less than one.

For example, if the average number of mortalities for heart surgery at a hospital were 4 percent (proportion = .04), a P-chart would be "most useful":

1. When the number of surgeries in each subgroup were at least 50, or

2. when n (pBar) is greater than four.

The absolute minimum number of surgeries in each subgroup should be:

1. At least 25—or alternately,

2. n (pBar) should be greater than one.

This has important implications for identifying special causes. When the subgroup size is at least 50 (or alternately > 4/pBar), then a point above the UCL can be identified as a special cause with *confidence*. Otherwise, the "special cause" might be a false positive (Type-I error) due to skewness in the data. When this occurs, one solution would be to combine subgroups to get the minimum subgroup size needed. This approach is illustrated in the following case study of heart surgery mortality.

CASE STUDY: AN HMO EVALUATES ITS PROVIDERS FOR CABG SURGERY

Key Learning Points

1. Drilling down into aggregate data to improve a process (see chapter 3)

2. Subgrouping strategies for P-charts

The Situation

The Worldbest HMO has been allowing its members to use any one of four different hospitals for coronary artery bypass graft (CABG) surgery. There are no significant differences among the patients who go to the four hospitals with respect to age, gender, or risk factors. However, some have charged that the mortality has risen over the last four years. A P-chart was constructed to analyze the combined CABG mortality data for all four hospitals (Figure 5.3).

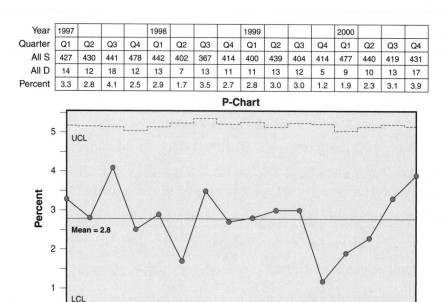

Year	1997				1998				1999				2000			
Quarter	Q1	Q2	Q3	Q4	Q1	Q2	Q3	Q4	Q1	Q2	Q3	Q4	Q1	Q2	Q3	Q4
All S	427	430	441	478	442	402	367	414	400	439	404	414	477	440	419	431
All D	14	12	18	12	13	7	13	11	11	13	12	5	9	10	13	17
Percent	3.3	2.8	4.1	2.5	2.9	1.7	3.5	2.7	2.8	3.0	3.0	1.2	1.9	2.3	3.1	3.9

Figure 5.3   CABG mortality aggregated for four hospitals: quarters from 1997–2000.

Questions

1. Why were quarterly data chosen for analysis, rather than yearly data?

2. Were there any special causes?

3. What should be the next step if the HMO wished to see this process improved?

Analysis and Interpretation

1. Quarterly data were chosen because it is desirable to have about 20 subgroups for a solid chart. Yearly data would have provided only four points. Using the ASTM formula, 4/pBar (or 4/.028), there should be a minimum of 143 cases per subgroups for a solid chart. Figure 5.3 shows that quarterly subgroups average over 400, more than enough for a useful P-chart. Notice that both the UCL and LCL appear on this chart and there are no percentages equal to zero. Therefore, quarterly data provide a strong P-chart.

2. There are no special causes. The "trend" of five consecutively ascending quarters in 1999–2000 is one short of being a special cause. The capability of this process over the four hospitals can only tentatively be described as averaging 2.8 percent because we do not have the required minimum of 20 points needed to estimate the capability with confidence. (Recall from the previous chapter that *only the mean* can be used to estimate process capability with stair-stepped limits.)

3. If the HMO wished to improve this process, then they should stratify the data by hospital and compare the four hospitals on the same control chart using rational ordering.

The Next Step

First, the four hospitals presented their data to the HMO management in tabular form (Table 5.1). Hospital A claimed that it deserved to be ranked "number one" because its mortality rate over the last four years (2.2 percent) was 30 percent lower than Hospitals B and C, and 60 percent lower than Hospital D. Hospital A also cited the data in Table 5.1 to show that Hospital B's mortality rate showed a "sharp upward trend" during 2000 because its mortality rate had increased over four consecutive quarters. Hospital B and C disagreed, saying that their mortality rates (3.2 percent and 3.1 percent respectively) were not statistically different from Hospital A (using Chi-square analysis not shown here). Hospital D acknowledged that its rate (6.7 percent) was higher than the other hospitals, but argued that it had "greatly improved" during the last two years because it had no mortalities in four of the last eight quarters.

To clarify the disputed interpretation of Table 5.1, the HMO management had the same data analyzed on a control chart using rational ordering (Figure 5.4).

Questions

4. What can you learn from Figure 5.4? Should Hospital A be ranked the "best" among these four hospitals as they claimed?

5. Did Hospital B have an upward "trend" in mortality during 2000?

6. Has Hospital D "greatly improved" over the past two years?

Analysis and Interpretation

4. Figure 5.4 shows that neither Hospital A, B, or C were special causes within this system of four hospitals. (The tenth quarter for Hospital B was just under the UCL.) Their average mortality rates are not demonstrably different from each other. However, Hospital A's performance is somewhat better from the standpoint that its mortality rate shows *less variability* than Hospital B, C, and D. It also performs more surgeries.

   However, Hospital D had two quarters in 2000 that are above the UCL—a special cause! Also, notice that Hospital D had no mortalities in six quarters, a signal that its data are skewed due to the small number of surgeries. Using the formula 4/pBar (4/.028), Hospital D is far short of the 142 cases per quarter needed for a solid chart. In fact, it does not really have the absolute minimum number of surgeries for a useful chart based on quarterly data (1/pBar—or 1/.028 = 36 cases minimum). Therefore, the special cause might be due to skewness in the data.

Table 5.1 CABG mortality data for four hospitals (quarters of 1997–2000).

Quarter		Hospital A			Hospital B			Hospital C			Hospital D		
		Deaths	Surgeries		Deaths	Surgeries		Deaths	Surgeries		Deaths	Surgeries	
1997	Q1	4	199	2.0%	6	126	4.8%	4	88	4.5%	0	14	0.0%
	Q2	3	204	1.5%	2	121	1.7%	5	90	5.6%	2	15	13.3%
	Q3	5	194	2.6%	9	140	6.4%	3	89	3.4%	1	18	5.6%
	Q4	6	232	2.6%	3	123	2.4%	1	100	1.0%	2	23	8.7%
1998	Q1	7	212	3.3%	4	110	3.6%	1	97	1.0%	1	23	4.3%
	Q2	3	199	1.5%	2	110	1.8%	2	82	2.4%	0	11	0.0%
	Q3	6	201	3.0%	3	76	3.9%	3	77	3.9%	1	13	7.7%
	Q4	4	219	1.8%	1	92	1.1%	4	83	4.8%	2	20	10.0%
1999	Q1	8	242	3.3%	0	78	0.0%	3	70	4.3%	0	10	0.0%
	Q2	3	271	1.1%	7	89	7.9%	3	70	4.3%	0	9	0.0%
	Q3	7	250	2.8%	2	71	2.8%	2	73	2.7%	1	10	10.0%
	Q4	4	265	1.5%	0	69	0.0%	1	65	1.5%	0	15	0.0%
2000	Q1	3	298	1.0%	0	85	0.0%	3	74	4.1%	3	20	15.0%
	Q2	6	251	2.4%	2	100	2.0%	2	72	2.8%	0	17	0.0%
	Q3	6	258	2.3%	4	95	4.2%	2	52	3.8%	1	14	7.1%
	Q4	9	268	3.4%	5	68	7.4%	0	75	0.0%	3	20	15.0%
Totals		**84**	**3763**	**2.2%**	**50**	**1553**	**3.2%**	**39**	**1257**	**3.1%**	**17**	**252**	**6.7%**

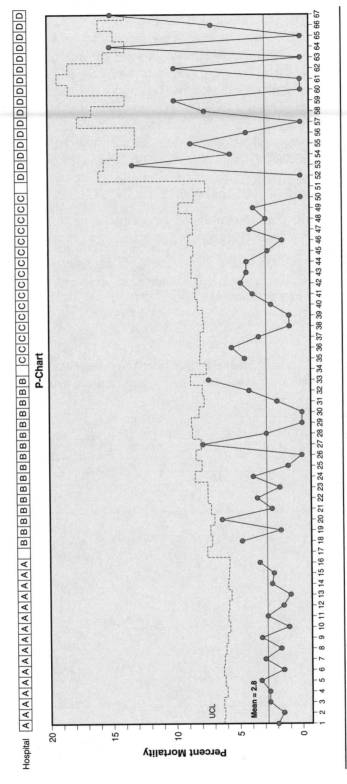

Figure 5.4   Rational ordering of four hospitals: quarterly data for 1997–2000 CABG mortality.

In order to be certain that Hospital D is really a special cause with respect to the other three hospitals, it is necessary to combine all the data for each hospital into four *rational subgroups*—and analyze the data not in a time-ordered design, but using a cross-sectional comparison (Figure 5.5). Figure 5.5 clearly shows that Hospital D is a special cause within this group of four hospitals. This is a solid P-chart because all four hospitals have more than 142 surgeries (4/pbar = 4/.028). Notice that the data points are no longer joined because we are looking at a cross-sectional comparison, not a time-ordered control chart. Finally, observe that even with this powerful chart, Hospital A is still not a special cause within this group of four hospitals, that is, its performance is still above its LCL.

5. Figure 5.4 shows that Hospital B did not have an upward "trend" during 2000 because four consecutively ascending points are not a "trend."

6. Both Table 5.1 and Figure 5.4 show that Hospital D had not "greatly improved" over the 1999–2000 period. It had no mortalities in four of the eight quarters because it had a small number of surgeries!

Question

7. If Hospitals B, C, or D wished to introduce improvement plans in January 2001, how would they assess the effectiveness of these plans?

Hospital	A	B	C	D
Years	1997–2000	1997–2000	1997–2001	1997–2002
Surgeries	3763	1553	1257	252
Deaths	84	50	39	17
Percent	2.2	3.2	3.1	6.7

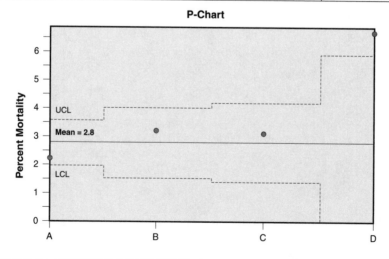

Figure 5.5 **Rational subgrouping of four hospitals: yearly subgroups from 1997–2000.** CABG mortality.

Analysis and Interpretation

7. Hospitals B, C, and D should construct *separate* control charts for each of their hospitals and continue to use (that is, lock in) their previous centerlines based on the 1997–2000 data. Technically, it would be better to have at least 20 subgroups with only common cause variation before locking in the centerline. But 16 points provide a reasonable baseline for comparison.

   Figure 5.6 illustrates how a separate chart for Hospital B would look. Hospital B's chart would be most useful if each subgroup had at least 125 surgeries (4/pBar = 4/.032). Notice that when the subgroups fall below this 125, "zero percent" appears three times—signaling a weakening of the chart due to skewness in the data.

Management Considerations

The HMO can learn a great deal about mortalities from these data. For example, they might ask themselves whether the number of surgeries done at a hospital has an effect on overall patient safety and survival. Should specialized surgeries, such as CABG surgery, be assigned to one of the four hospitals as a method of reducing mortality rates? Should a hospital be required to do a minimum number of specialized surgeries—or do none at all?

Quarter	Q1	Q2	Q3	Q4	Q1	Q2	Q3	Q4	Q1	Q2	Q3	Q4	Q1	Q2	Q3	Q4	Q1	Q2	Q3	Q4
Surgeries	126	121	140	123	110	110	76	92	78	89	71	69	85	100	95	68				
Deaths	6	2	9	3	4	2	3	1	0	7	2	0	0	2	4	4				
Percent	4.8	1.7	6.4	2.4	3.6	1.8	3.9	1.1	0.0	7.9	2.8	0.0	0.0	2.0	4.2	5.9				

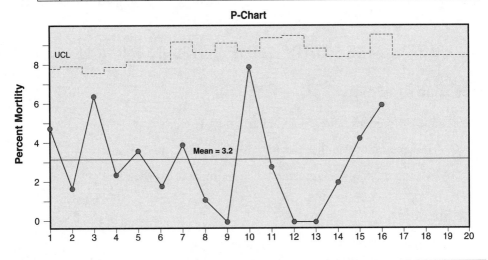

Figure 5.6   Hospital B—showing 1997–2000 baseline—CABG mortality.
Data for the following quarters will be compared to previous baseline. Hospital B should have a minimum of 31 surgeries per quarter (1/pBar) for a useful chart.

The Board and medical staff at Hospital D need to address serious questions before allowing CABG surgery to proceed. Are they doing enough CABG surgeries to continue to offer this type of surgery? Have the problems been identified and addressed in an improvement plan? Is it enough to show that they will have improved over their previous performance? Or should the target be set at the level of performance of the other hospitals? (Setting goals and targets will be discussed in chapter 6.)

Subgroup Sizes for C-Charts and U-Charts

Recall that C-charts and U-charts measure nonconformities, rather than nonconforming items. The U-chart is the chart of choice when the "area of opportunity" varies from time period to time period. The C-chart is used when the "area of opportunity" is approximately equal from period to period.

The formula suggested by the ASTM for determining the subgroup sample size for U-charts and C-charts is similar to the one described above for the P-chart.[5] The ASTM suggests that, to provide reliable information, the subgroup size for a *U-chart* should *at least* be equal to one divided by the average of nonconformities ("uBar"). However, the U-chart will be *most useful* when the subgroup size is at least equal to four divided by uBar. For example, if the average number of medication errors at a hospital is four per 1000 (or 0.004), the U-chart would be most useful when the subgroup size (that is, the number of medication orders) was at least 4/0.004 or 1000. When the subgroup size equals at least 4/uBar, then a point above the UCL can be identified as a special cause with confidence. On the other hand, when the subgroup size is smaller than 1/uBar, then a U-chart may not provide any reliable information.

Finally, the subgroup size for the *C-chart* should be large enough that the average count of nonconforming items (cBar) is at least greater than one, but preferably greater than four. The application of this formula is illustrated in the following case study.

CASE STUDY: CODE BLUES IN THE ICU

Key Learning Points

1. The differences between a C-chart and a U-chart

2. The amount of data needed for subgroups in C- and U-charts

3. Drilling down into aggregated data to improve a process

The Situation

A nurse had worked in the intensive care unit (ICU) of a hospital from May to December 1994. During that period the nurse was also the head of the hospital's Code Blue team (that responds to patients experiencing cardiac arrest). Subsequent to leaving the hospital, he was hired by a nursing home after having received a very positive recommendation from the hospital. However, within six months of working at the nursing home the nurse was arrested and later convicted of causing the death of a resident by putting potassium chloride into the resident's medication. During the trial the nurse admitted that he had done the same thing to patients when he was employed at the hospital. As a result, charges were also brought against the hospital on the grounds that it should have known of the nurse's criminal behavior.

The director of quality improvement at the hospital responded that she had routinely monitored Code Blue data. Although she had noticed an increase in Code Blues during the time of the nurse's employment at the hospital, her analysis showed that the increase had not been "statistically significant." (She had used the Chi-square statistic to analyze the ICU code blues comparing the first six months with the last six months of 1994.) However, at this time the director reanalyzed the Code Blue data using four control charts and a Pareto chart:

- A U-chart: for all six units (ICU, ED, two surgical units, and two medical units) taken together (Figure 5.7)

- A C-chart for the same data (Figure 5.8)

- A Pareto chart showing the location of the Code Blues (Figure 5.9)

- A U-chart for the ICU data alone ((Figure 5.10)

- A C-chart for the ICU (Figure 5.11)

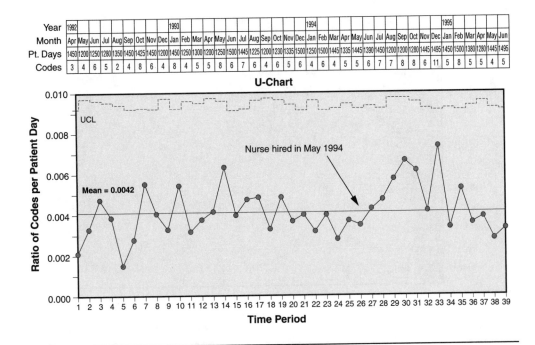

Figure 5.7   Ratio of Code Blues per patient day—all units.
Number of patient days per subgroup should be > 4/uBar (4/.0042) = 952.

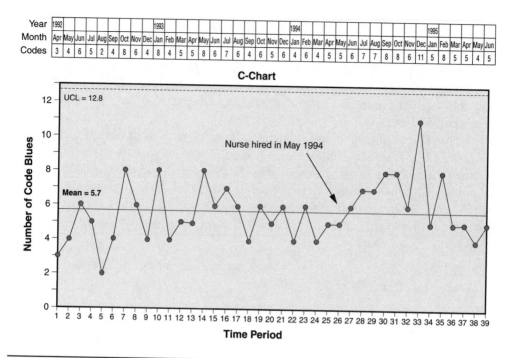

Figure 5.8   Number of Code Blues per month—all units.

Number of Code Blues per month should be > 4.

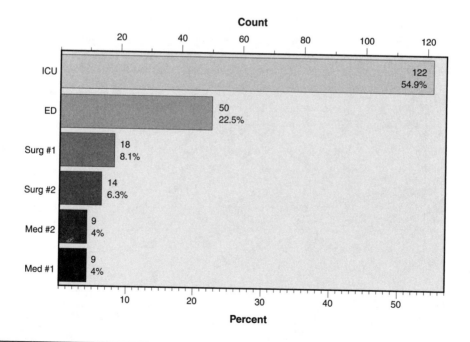

Figure 5.9   Pareto chart showing location of Code Blues (1992–1995)—total counts.

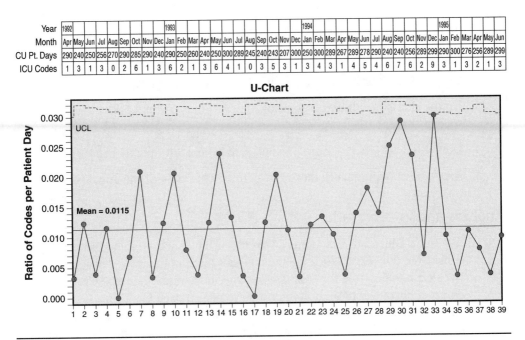

Year	1992									1993												1994													1995				
Month	Apr	May	Jun	Jul	Aug	Sep	Oct	Nov	Dec	Jan	Feb	Mar	Apr	May	Jun	Jul	Aug	Sep	Oct	Nov	Dec	Jan	Feb	Mar	Apr	May	Jun	Jul	Aug	Sep	Oct	Nov	Dec	Jan	Feb	Mar	Apr	May	Jun
CU Pt. Days	290	240	250	256	270	290	285	290	240	290	250	260	240	250	300	289	245	240	243	207	300	250	300	289	267	289	278	290	240	240	256	289	299	290	300	276	256	289	299
ICU Codes	1	3	1	3	0	2	6	1	3	6	2	1	3	6	4	1	0	3	5	3	1	3	4	3	1	4	5	4	6	7	6	2	9	3	1	3	2	1	3

Figure 5.10   ICU codes per patient day—monthly data.

Number of patient days per subgroup should ideally be > 4/uBar (4/.011) = 267.

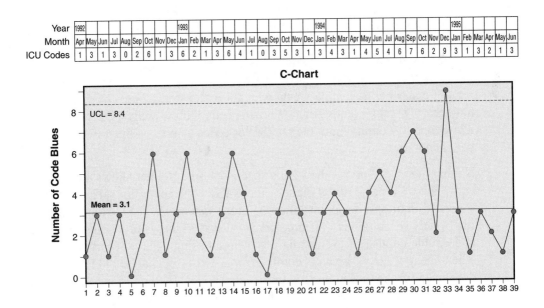

Year	1992									1993												1994													1995				
Month	Apr	May	Jun	Jul	Aug	Sep	Oct	Nov	Dec	Jan	Feb	Mar	Apr	May	Jun	Jul	Aug	Sep	Oct	Nov	Dec	Jan	Feb	Mar	Apr	May	Jun	Jul	Aug	Sep	Oct	Nov	Dec	Jan	Feb	Mar	Apr	May	Jun
ICU Codes	1	3	1	3	0	2	6	1	3	6	2	1	3	6	4	1	0	3	5	3	1	3	4	3	1	4	5	4	6	7	6	2	9	3	1	3	2	1	3

Figure 5.11   ICU codes per month (C-chart).

Mean number of Code Blues per month should ideally be > 4, but not less than 1.

Questions

1. Why were a C- and U-chart chosen to analyze these data?

2. How do the C- and U-charts differ? Which is more appropriate for these data?

3. Do the charts for all units taken together (Figures 5.7 and 5.8) show any special causes?

4. Do the ICU charts (Figures 5.10 and 5.11) show any special causes?

5. Are there enough data in these charts to be confident of the conclusions?

Analysis and Interpretation

1. The Code Blue data are counts of events or incidences and therefore are considered count (or "attribute") data—not measurement (or "variable") data. Because it is possible for a patient to experience more than one Code Blue during a hospitalization, it is important to regard each Code as a "nonconformity," rather than as a "nonconforming item." Because the number of patient days differs from month to month, the "area of opportunity" also differs. Therefore, it is appropriate to track the ratio of all nonconformities per patient day on a U-chart.

2. One could also use a C-chart in place of a U-chart when the area of opportunity (that is, patient days) is approximately the same from period to period (that is, when the number for each month does not vary by more than 20 percent from the average number of patient days). Figure 5.7 reveals this to be the case because the total number of patient days for all units ranges from 1200 to 1500. Therefore, either chart is a correct choice. Some might prefer the C-chart because it analyzes the actual number of codes, rather than the ratio of codes per patient day. Others might prefer to use both charts. Using both charts together lends additional perspective to the analysis, because it allows one to examine both the number of codes as well as the ratio of codes per patient day.

3. Neither Figure 5.7 or 5.8 shows any special causes. Neither shows a point above the UCL nor a run of eight or more above the centerline. (The U-chart shows a run of only six points after the nurse was hired. The C-chart shows a run of only seven points.) A common cause system that is producing an undesirable number of events might be studied using a Pareto chart to see where most of the variation is coming from. A control chart should then be developed for the unit or units with the most codes. In this instance, the Pareto chart (Figure 5.9) was unnecessary because the ICU had already been identified as the potential problem. Nevertheless, the Pareto chart clearly shows that the ICU unit had the predominant number of the Code Blues.

4. Both the U-chart (Figure 5.10) and the C-chart (Figure 5.11) analyzing the ICU data show a special cause. Both have a single point (December 1994)

above the UCL. This demonstrates that either the C- or the U-chart would have been an appropriate choice for a chart.

It is best to exercise caution in concluding that a special cause exists when the amount of data is limited. Using the ASTM formula, a U-chart will be most useful when uBar (that is, the mean or centerline) times the number in each time period is four or more. When this product is less than one, the control chart may not yield reliable information. If the number is between one and four, one can be confident of the results if only common cause variation is present. In the present case, the average ICU patient days per month is approximately 290, which when multiplied by the mean (.011) is slightly less than four. The mean of the C-chart is also slightly less than four. Therefore, the special cause identified might be due to the slight skewness of the data distribution. In order to confirm the presence of a special cause, it is advisable to combine the monthly subgroups into bimonthly subgroups (Figure 5.12).

Questions

6. Does the C-chart with bimonthly subgroups (Figure 5.12) confirm the presence of a special cause?

7. Should the hospital have been aware of a potential problem with increased codes in the ICU and investigated the nature of the problem?

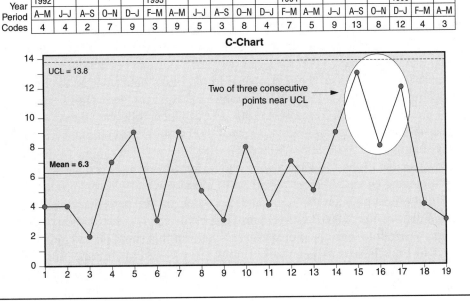

Year	1992				1993						1994				1995		
Period	A–M	J–J	A–S	O–N	D–J	F–M	A–M	J–J	A–S	O–N	D–J	F–M	A–M	J–J	A–S	O–N	D–J	F–M	A–M
Codes	4	4	2	7	9	3	9	5	3	8	4	7	5	9	13	8	12	4	3

C-Chart

UCL = 13.8

Two of three consecutive points near UCL

Mean = 6.3

Figure 5.12 Bimonthly analysis of ICU Code Blues (C-chart).
Mean number of Code Blues per subgroup is > 4.

Analysis and Interpretation

6. Yes, the C-chart with bimonthly subgroups confirms the presence of a special cause. In December 1994, one can observe the presence of two of three consecutive data points near the UCL, that is, above the two-sigma line (not shown). The mean (6.3) is greater than four, which allows for a confident conclusion that a special cause is present.

7. Yes, the hospital should have been aware of a potential problem in the ICU and investigated the root cause of the problem. However, this is one instance in which the addition of the "zones" (that is, the one and two sigma lines) in Figure 5.12 might have helped those less skilled in the use of control charts recognize that two of three consecutive points were beyond two sigmas.

Management Considerations

This case study illustrates two important issues for management. First, it is important to look at data over time, rather than do static comparisons (for example, Chi-square tests) between one time period and another. Second, common cause variation doesn't always mean that a process is functioning at an acceptable level. To improve common cause variation, one should disaggregate the data by drilling down into organizational units or stratifying the data in some other appropriate manner.

MONITORING "RARE EVENTS"

The question is sometimes asked about how to monitor "rare events." What kind of chart should be used? How large should the subgroups be? The answer really depends on the size of the "area of opportunity." For example, how should a department of anesthesiology monitor bronchospasms during anesthesia that occur 200 times a year in a large hospital that does about 25,000 surgeries per year? This can be monitored with several different charts. Of course, the first choice for *binomial* data (that is, the event either occurred or it did not) is a P-chart (see chapter 2). The average overall yearly percentage for bronchospasms is 0.8 percent (200/25,000). Then, following the ASTM formula for determining the subgroup size (4/pBar = 4/.008 = 500), one could use a P-chart with weekly subgroups (25,000/500 = 50 weeks).

However, the C-chart is often a good choice for rare events when the area of opportunity (potential events) is large. Grant and Leavenworth (1988) point out that as the value of the denominator increases and the value of the percentage decreases, the *binomial* distribution of the P-charts approximates the *Poisson* distribution of the C- and U-charts.[6] Therefore, one could also use a C-chart for this situation and merely plot the number of bronchospasms per week. Following the ASTM formula, subgroups for C-charts should average about four. In this case weekly subgroups will work well (200/52 = 3.85), which is sufficiently close to four to provide a useful chart.

As was discussed in the beginning of this chapter, Wheeler's recommendation of plotting the percentage of bronchospasms on an I-chart would also work because the numbers in the denominators are large. In this case weekly subgroup size would be about 500. In summary, with rare events and a very large potential for the event to occur, the P-, C-, or I-chart would have a similar pattern and interpretation.

Consider another situation in which you cannot accurately estimate the area of opportunity, although you know it is very large. For example, the safety committee might want to monitor needle sticks. The opportunity for these events is large, but cannot be determined with precision. Even in this case, the data will take on a Poisson distribution and one can safely use a C-chart (Grant and Leavenworth 1988).[7]

Now consider the situation where the rare events occur in a small area of opportunity. For example, suppose you want to monitor the number of clinical complications (such as wound infections, returns to the operating room, and so on) in bowel operations at a hospital that only performs about 200 bowel operations per year. The percentage of any of these complications is less than 2 percent. It will take a long time to get enough subgroups to monitor these complications because any one of these complications will occur only about four times a year!

In such a situation in which you have a *very* rare event, you can use the strategy of changing *count* data into *measurement* data and plotting the measurements on an I-chart. How is this done? It is done by measuring the number of "successes between failures" and plotting the number of successful surgeries between patients who had *one or more* complications. Each subgroup on the I-chart will be the number of "successes" between a "failure." The next case study will illustrate how this is done.

CASE STUDY: EVALUATING A BOWEL SURGERY PATHWAY

The Situation

A hospital was losing money on bowel surgery patients reimbursed through Medicare (patients over 65 years of age). An improvement team was formed whose goal was to reduce "utilization of resources" without "detriment to clinical care." A stratification approach was employed in order to achieve "risk adjustment." The team decided to focus only on patients who:

- Were undergoing *elective* bowel surgery (that is, non-emergency patients)

- Were having a *single* procedure

- Were 65 years of age and older

About 10 patients per month met the above description.

Next the team had to decide on *operational definitions* for "use of resources" and "clinical complications." They settled on "post-operative length of stay (LOS)" as a proxy measure of utilization of resources. A definition of clinical complications was more difficult. The team decided on five clinical complications, each of which occurs about 1 or 2 percent of the time. The data for each complication were easy to obtain from the information system. The complications included:

- Wound infection
- Return to the OR during the same hospital stay
- Pulmonary embolism
- Pneumonia
- Readmission to the hospital for the same problem in less than 30 days

Questions

1. The team used I-charts to analyze LOS with monthly subgroups (Figures 5.13 and 5.14). Was this the best chart?

2. Based on these charts, was the pathway successful in reducing utilization of resources?

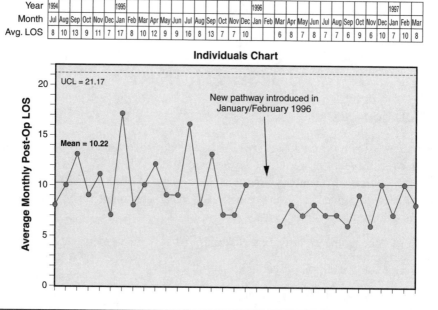

Figure 5.13   Bowel surgery post-operative LOS (patients 65 and older).
I-chart shows effect of new pathway on resource utilization. Mean LOS from baseline period is extended when new pathway is introduced.

Analysis and Interpretation

1. Length of stay (LOS) is measurement data. Ideally, an X-bar and S-chart should have been used. The S-chart would have provided information on the consistency of LOS *within* each month, while the X-bar chart would have shown whether or not the process LOS had changed over time. In fact, the team decided to use an easier approach to data collection and kept track of the average LOS for each month. The monthly averages were then plotted on an I-chart. This decision is acceptable, but the X-bar and S-chart would have been a better choice.

2. Yes, the new pathway was effective in reducing post-operative LOS. Figure 5.13 shows that the mean LOS before the pathway was 10.22 days. The centerline was extended (locked in) at the time the new pathway was introduced. The LOS for the next 11 months after the introduction of the pathway were all below the baseline mean—more than enough to meet the test of eight or more points required for a special cause. Figure 5.14 then replots the same data to show the capability of the process before and after the pathway. Before the pathway, the mean was 10.22 days with a UCL of 21 days. (The LCL defaulted to zero.) Afterward, the mean of the process was 7.62 days with a UCL of 13 days and an LCL of about two days. The LOS had been reduced about 30 percent and the process was much more predictable, as demonstrated by the narrower control limits.

Year	1994						1995												1996												1997		
Month	Jul	Aug	Sep	Oct	Nov	Dec	Jan	Feb	Mar	Apr	May	Jun	Jul	Aug	Sep	Oct	Nov	Dec	Jan	Feb	Mar	Apr	May	Jun	Jul	Aug	Sep	Oct	Nov	Dec	Jan	Feb	Mar
Avg. LOS	8	10	13	9	11	7	17	8	10	12	9	9	16	8	13	7	7	10			6	8	7	8	7	7	6	9	6	10	7	10	8

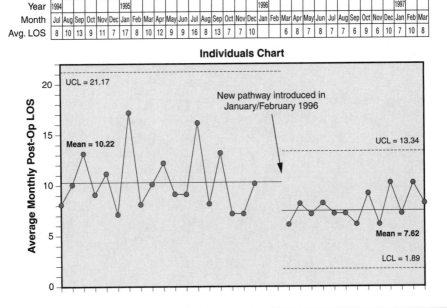

Individuals Chart

Figure 5.14   Bowel surgery post-operative LOS—before and after new pathway.
Chart shows process capability before and after new pathway.

Questions

3. The team used an I-chart to analyze clinical complications by measuring the number of successful surgeries between patients who had one or more of the five complications (Figure 5.15). Why did they use a single I-chart to analyze these complications, rather than use a separate P-chart for each of the five complications?

4. What was the effect of the initial pathway on clinical outcomes? Were six subgroups enough to identify a special cause? Why didn't the team wait longer before revising the pathway?

5. Were the clinical outcomes after the revision of the pathway as good as the initial baseline of care?

Analysis and Interpretation

3. There was not sufficient data to generate separate P-charts for each complication. Using the ASTM formula, you would need 50 to 200 surgeries in each subgroup based on a two percent incidence rate. You would need between one and four complications in each subgroup to generate separate C-charts. Therefore, the team transformed the count data into measurement data by counting the number of successful surgeries between patients who had one or more complications.

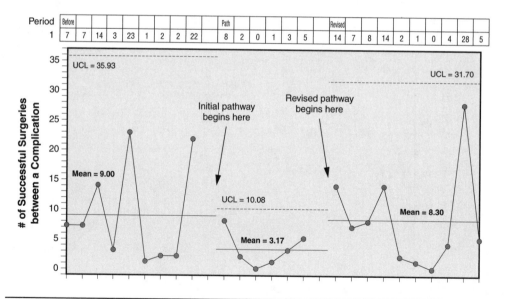

Figure 5.15   Effect of bowel surgery pathway on clinical outcomes.
An example of converting count data into measurement data. Each point shows a patient with one or more of five possible complications.

4. The introduction of the pathway in January 1996 seemed to have a negative effect. The next six points were all below the baseline mean of nine successful surgeries between complications. Because the safety of patients was at stake, the team did not wait for a run of eight. They chose to ignore the high probability of Type-I error (identifying a false special cause). In fact, the team's investigation revealed both a weakness in the pathway and a failure to implement one aspect of the pathway according to plan. First, they found that the "window" for the administration of an antibiotic before surgery needed to be adjusted. Second, they found that in surgeries that lasted over three hours, antibiotics were not readministered—as the pathway called for.

5. When these changes were made, the average time between complications rose to a mean of 8.3 surgeries—which was almost as good as the initial baseline.

ENDNOTES

1. E. L. Grant and R. S. Leavenworth, *Statistical Quality Control* (New York: McGraw-Hill, 1988): 265.
2. D. J. Wheeler, *Advanced Topics in Statistical Process Control* (Knoxville, TN: SPC Press, 1995): 267.
3. D. C. Montgomery, *Introduction to Statistical Quality Control* (New York: John Wiley & Sons, 1991): 160–61.
4. American Society for Testing and Materials, *Manual on Presentation of Data and Control Chart Analysis* (Philadelphia: ASTM, 1995): 58.
5. Ibid, 59–61.
6. Grant and Leavenworth, *Statistical Quality Control,* 209–13.
7. Ibid, 213.

6

Obtaining Meaningful Data

Without meaningful data, control charts are nothing more than "chart junk." Control charts may be constructed in color with the best of software programs, but without meaningful data they will not help in knowing whether a process is improving or not. Selecting a few good indicators and developing a workable data collection plan will save both time and resources. Data collection is expensive. Unfortunately, not all data are useful. Therefore, in the first part of this chapter I will review some general principles of measurement, discuss various types of measures and two sampling methods, and offer some guidelines for developing indicators.

The second part of this chapter will address benchmarking and goal setting. Benchmarking is sometimes confused with obtaining useful comparison data and with goal setting. Obtaining appropriate comparison data and plotting goals on control charts can be helpful in analyzing the effectiveness of an improvement effort, as will be illustrated in chapter 8. It is often useful to think about goal setting at the time when indicators are developed. Therefore, it is logical to discuss this topic in the same chapter with indicator development.

GENERAL PRINCIPLES OF MEASUREMENT

Measurement can be thought of as a *window* through which we view a process. Each measure or indicator is a window that provides a different perspective on a process. Those windows should be as clear as possible. If the window is murky or cloudy, our vision is blurred. As a result, we may be lulled into thinking that our process is functioning at an adequate level and make no effort to improve it, when in reality it could and should be improved. On the other hand, cloudy windows might lead us to conclude that the time and resources we spent in improving a process were wasted, when in reality they were successful.

The measures we choose should focus on the process itself, not on people. In the introduction of this book, a distinction was drawn between measuring for judgment and measuring for improvement. Indicators needed for measuring process improvement are not the same as those needed for performance appraisal or for credentialing of physicians. Remembering this distinction will help remove the "threat" sometimes felt by the "owners" of the process we are trying to improve.

Measures need to be *actionable*. This means that measures should focus on something over which an improvement team has the power to effect a change. For example, there is no point in collecting data on "adequacy of staffing" unless someone has the authority and resources to make a change in staffing. Indicators should also be specific enough to provide guidance for improvement efforts. For example, if the only item on a patient satisfaction questionnaire asks a patient to rate "the overall quality of nursing care," it is difficult for the nurses to know exactly how they might respond to a poor rating. However, if patients were also asked to rate "satisfaction with the promptness with which the call button was answered," the nurse would have a clearer idea of which actions might help to improve satisfaction.

TYPES OF MEASURES

Measures can be categorized in different ways. It is helpful to keep the distinctions in mind when selecting or developing indicators. All will be useful at one time or another.

Domains of Quality

Indicators can be viewed from the standpoint of the *domain of quality* they address:

- Safety (for example, patient falls, medication errors)

- Clinical excellence or effectiveness (for example, did a new pathway achieve its goal?)

- Resource utilization or efficiency (for example, were ICU days or length of hospital stay reduced?)

- Timeliness (for example, was lab turnaround time reduced?)

- Accessibility (for example, how long does a patient wait to get an appointment?)

- Patient satisfaction (for example, are patients likely to recommend the hospital?)

Outcome versus Process Measures

Both *outcome* and *process* measures can be useful to measure success. For example, if the goal is to reduce ventilator-associated pneumonia (VAP) in the ICU by 25 percent within the current year, an outcome measure might be the VAP rate (the number of pneumonias per patient day). Examples of related process measures are length of intubation or reintubation rate.

Both outcome and process measures have their strengths and weaknesses. In healthcare, outcome measures can present a problem. Some evaluators are reluctant to use outcome measures because they require risk adjustment and it is difficult to obtain consensus on algorithms. It is also true that negative outcomes can happen even when "correct" procedures are followed and positive outcomes can occur even when they are not.

Process measures are early indicators of outcomes. They are selected by moving "upstream" and asking what might effect a change in a desired outcome. It is often easier to collect data on process indicators than on outcome indicators. They are useful when there is general agreement on the connection between the indicator and the outcome. For example, increasing immunization rates is a process indicator that is generally accepted as related to the outcome of reducing community-acquired pneumonia. Decreasing intubation time after surgery is generally accepted as one way to decrease ventilator-related pneumonia. Tracking the time between a patient's arrival in the emergency department with chest pain and the initiation of thrombolytic therapy is a useful process indicator because it is generally agreed that shortening this time will reduce the negative outcomes (for example, heart damage or mortality).

However, when both process and outcome measures are used together, they complement each other and provide a reasonably good window for viewing a process. The outcome of care is what patients are most interested in. Patients want to have their problems addressed, their symptoms ameliorated. They trust providers to do whatever is necessary to achieve a successful outcome. However, it is true that many outcomes, such as mortality, are largely determined by patient characteristics and preexisting conditions beyond physician control. Comparing outcomes without some type of risk adjustment can be misleading. However, the absence of risk adjustment need not impede efforts to evaluate outcome quality. Within a given setting (for example, hospital, outpatient site) it is reasonable to monitor outcomes over time for a specific disease or process unless patient characteristics change markedly. For example, one could monitor C-section rates at a given hospital on a monthly basis without having a complicated risk-adjustment system, as long as one can reasonably assume that the patient population is substantially the same from month to month. However, it would be inappropriate to compare C-section rates at a community hospital with the rate at a tertiary care facility without adjusting for risk.

Stratification can sometimes be an acceptable proxy for risk adjustment of outcomes. For example, some major centers for heart surgery have developed sophisticated risk-adjustment algorithms so that comparisons could be made among sites and surgeons. However, risk-adjustment systems are often problematic. They tend to be viewed as valid by the providers and sites that appear to do well, but not by those who have less successful results. Instead of risk adjustment, it is possible to stratify outcomes on the basis of variables that are generally recognized as influencing outcomes. For example, there are data to show that survival rates of heart surgery will be better for younger patients than for older patients, and for male patients than for females. Therefore, instead of arguing the validity of a risk-adjustment system and plotting risk-adjusted mortality on a single control chart, it might be better to generate four separate control charts: one for males under 65 years of age, a second for males 65 and older, a third for females under 65, and a fourth for females 65 and older. The obvious drawback of stratification is that it requires a larger patient population.

In practice, indicators must be credible to the "owners" of the process to be useful. The ultimate test of the validity of a measure is that the providers believe that they can use the data to improve. A process indicator will not be useful if the persons who own the process don't accept the connection between the process indicator and the outcome. Nor will an outcome measure be useful if the owners of the process don't accept your risk-adjustment algorithm or stratification method. The owners of the process must "buy-in" to your selection of indicators before you spend time and money collecting data on your indicators.

Continuous Measures versus Count Measures

Continuous measures are better than count measures. As was discussed in the last chapter, selecting indicators that can be measured, rather than counted, allows the construction of more powerful control charts. Continuous data can be plotted on variable charts, whereas count data are plotted on attribute charts. For example, suppose we want to measure the process indicator, reducing "door-to-drug time" in the emergency department, with the purpose of achieving a better outcome, namely, a reduction in mortality. It is not uncommon to measure this process indicator as *count* data, that is, either drug therapy was initiated within the targeted time of 30 minutes—or it was not. These data are binomial data and would be plotted on a P-chart, which would require a great deal of data (see chapter 5). However, if the *actual time* between patient admission and initiation of drug therapy were recorded for each patient, these data are *measurement* data. Measurement data are plotted on an I-chart—a more powerful chart, requiring fewer patients and less time than collecting count data for a P-chart.

SAMPLING METHODS

At the time you are selecting indicators and planning data collection, it is helpful to think about whether you wish to use sampling—and if so, which sampling plan you will use.

First, you should not sample if sufficient data for your study is easily available electronically. For example, if you plan to analyze C-section rates, there is no need for sampling. Every hospital has data readily available in its information system regarding the number of deliveries and the number of C-sections categorized by time-period, by type of C-section, by physician, and perhaps by other variables as well. Sampling is both unnecessary and undesirable.

On the other hand, never collect more data than you must to accomplish your purpose. Sampling can save time and money. Although there are many kinds of sampling, I want to single out two types that will be useful.

Stratified Random Sampling

First, suppose that you want to identify the main opportunities for improving patient satisfaction. Your goal is to take a "snapshot" of sources of dissatisfaction of patients discharged during the last three months. To do this, you need to conduct a patient survey that allows you to generalize your findings from an unbiased sample of patients to all patients discharged in the last three months. In this situation, *stratified random sampling* will be a good choice. Using a sampling table, you will select a random sample from each of the types ("strata") of patients of interest to you (for example, medical, surgical, pediatric, and so on).

Another situation in which you might use stratified random sampling is estimating the cycle time for all lab tests from a sample. For example, let us suppose that the Emergency Department (ED) is complaining that turnaround time (TAT) of lab tests is "terrible." You may want to take a sample of lab tests and generalize your findings to all ED lab tests; that is, you want to take a "snapshot" of cycle time and make an unbiased judgment about how "terrible" TAT actually is. Given a situation where the lab handles about 3000 lab requests per month from the ED, it is not feasible to measure TAT for 3000 tests to get a "snapshot." Instead, you need to take a stratified proportionate random sample. You would take a random sample determined by (that is, proportionate to) the number of different tests—and also by other variables of interest, such as day of week or shift. From the data gathered you would be able to estimate the TAT using descriptive statistics (for example, mean, standard deviation, standard error of the mean, and confidence limits). Your goal in this situation is to generalize your findings to all tests—and to do so with a minimum of bias.

Rational Sampling

On the other hand, if you are planning to assess process improvement on a control chart, *rational* or *judgment* sampling will save you time and money. Let us suppose that the result of the above study showed that the worst TAT was for tests requested during the day shift on weekdays. You want to implement an "improvement plan" and see whether the plan will be effective over the next few months. Using rational sampling, you could choose a few tests each weekday (I would recommend a number between four and seven), even though the total number of all tests was very large—and measure the TAT in minutes. Your goal is not to generalize your findings to all the tests for a given day, but to see whether the day shift process changes over time. You will have an unknown amount of bias in each daily sample. You will be taking small repeated samples from a process over time. Ideally you should sample for 20 to 25 days before introducing your improvement plan, and then about the same number of days afterward. If the first 20 days revealed common cause variation, then you could use the mean and control limits as a baseline against which to measure improvement. Rational sampling was illustrated in the example of lab test TAT in chapter 4, Figure 4.5 (page 61).

The main idea to keep in mind when using rational sampling is this: *Never knowingly subgroup unlike things together.* Each subgroup must be logically homogeneous.

This is why it is useful to keep samples small (four to seven), because this helps keep subgroups homogeneous and provides more power for detecting change between groups over time. Small samples will minimize variation within each subgroup and maximize the opportunity to detect change between subgroups over time.

One final thought. Keep in mind that rational sampling is a technique that is only used with measurement data that are analyzed on X-bar and S-charts or on X-bar and R-charts. You would not use rational sampling with I-charts (which are individual measurements) or with attribute charts.

Rational *ordering* and rational *subgrouping*—as distinguished from rational *sampling*—were explained in chapter 3 and illustrated in the case study on CABG surgery in chapter 5. In this study, mortality rates at four hospitals were first compared by rationally ordering quarterly data (Figure 5.4, page 79) and then by comparing the hospitals with mortality rates with four years of data subgrouped together (Figure 5.5, page 80). No sampling procedure was needed because all the data were available. As was also explained in chapter 3, rational *ordering* can be used with all control charts. Rational *subgrouping* cannot be used with I-charts, because by definition each point on an I-chart represents a *single* observation.

GUIDELINES FOR DEVELOPING INDICATORS

A multidimensional approach to measuring a process is recommended. This is sometimes referred to as developing a "family of measures." You may want one or more indicators to cover the various domains of measurement you feel are important for the process you are trying to improve: for example, clinical effectiveness, efficiency, safety, timeliness, and so on. The following steps are suggested for developing each indicator:

1. What aspect (*quality characteristic*) of this process will this indicator measure?

2. *Review the literature.* What indicators were used in other studies? Were these indicators used for basic research? Or have they been used for process improvement? Could you refine previous efforts and design a better indicator? Next, investigate whether previous teams in your organization have studied the same process. Other facilities in your healthcare system may be of help. Or other facilities with whom you have contact. If you find indicators used in previous studies acceptable to your goals, results of their studies may be useful to use as comparison data—to set goals for your process improvement effort.

   If you plan to obtain feedback from patients, search the literature to find a questionnaire that has documented validity and reliability. This will save time and money as compared to developing a new questionnaire (See chapter 7 for more on the topic of validity and reliability of survey questionnaires.)

3. What will be the *operational definition* of this indicator? The importance of clearly defining the operational definition of an indicator was discussed in chapter 1. The time to give thought to how an indicator will be quantified or

"operationally defined" is when you are deciding on whether or not to use it. For example, how do you plan to quantify "perioperative mortality?" "medication error?" "patient fall?" "wound infection?" "turnaround time?" It is not important that you use the same definition used in another study, unless you want the data from the other study for comparison data.

4. Develop a *data collection plan*. What is the source for your data? Answering the questions of "who? what? when? where? how?" may be helpful in choosing from a list of possible indicators. Is the data collection plan feasible? Do you have the budget and staff to collect data on this indicator? It is always best if you can obtain the data on your indicators from a database in your information system. If you have to develop new data collection instruments, such as checklists, and then train staff to use them, this will add to the cost of your study.[1]

   Does your indicator require data to be collected through a phone survey or a personal interview? This method will be more costly than a mailed survey or one that is distributed by hand. Do you have the necessary resources?

   Over what period of time do you need to collect data? Will you have enough staff, and sufficiently trained staff, to collect data on your indicator(s) over the proposed time period?

5. Will sampling be required? If so, describe your sampling plan in detail.

6. What is your plan for analysis and reporting of results?

   - Which graphs will be used?

   - Which control chart is the best for this indicator?

   - Do you have baseline data for this indicator? Where did it come from? Describe it.

   - Is there a target or goal for this indicator? Where did it come from? Is it an arbitrary numerical goal? Or is there a method and plan by which this goal is to be achieved?

At the end of this chapter, Exhibit 6.1 will present a sample indicator development form that can be used as a guide by a process improvement team. Exhibit 6.2 will present some sample indicators—resource consumption, clinical quality, and patient satisfaction—that might be appropriate for various specialties within a department of surgery.

BENCHMARKING

Leadership often expects that targets and goals be set for a process improvement effort. Goal setting is sometimes referred to as "benchmarking." However, the concept of benchmarking is different from either "obtaining comparison data" or "goal setting."

What Is Benchmarking?

The concept of benchmarking was popularized by Robert Camp (1989). His working definition is "the search for industry best practices that lead to superior performance."[2] Benchmarking requires an organization to obtain an external view to foster correctness of objective setting. It demands a constant testing of internal actions against external standards. Benchmarks show the direction that an organization must pursue rather than provide specific operationally quantifiable measures to be achieved in the immediate future. It is precisely in this focus that benchmarks differ from "targets." Targets are more precise and seek to quantify what should be achieved through benchmarking. "The significant difference between a complete benchmark definition and a target is that carefully conducted benchmark investigations will not only show what the benchmark metric is but also how it will be achieved."[3]

Is it true that Deming was opposed to benchmarking? Not really. Deming never said that organizations should ignore what competitors are doing. He did, however, warn against *blind copying* of competitors and advocated learning by developing good theories. He wrote, "If anyone were to study without theory such a company, that is, without knowing what questions to ask, he would be tempted to copy the company, on the pretext that 'they must be doing some things right.' To copy is to invite disaster."[4] Deming's comments do not imply that one should not study competitors and their practices but that to do so productively requires a theory by which to interpret their practices.

Identifying the "Best"

How can a healthcare provider decide who "the best" is?

One notable effort to identify best providers in healthcare is the HCIA annual reports. Since 1993, HCIA-Sachs, a Baltimore-based health information company, has compiled annually what it considers the top 100 hospitals nationwide—based on publicly available clinical and financial performance data among hospitals of various sizes and types. However, only two of their seven criteria (risk-adjusted mortality index and risk-adjusted complications index) deal with clinical issues. The other criteria deal mainly with financial issues (length of stay, expense per adjusted discharge, profitability, proportion of outpatient revenue, and total facility occupancy). Using these criteria to find "the best" hospitals in a category is problematic because of the heavy weight on financial and operational factors and comparatively less weight on clinical factors.

A *Wall Street Journal* article examined the claims of health maintenance organizations (HMOs) about their high rankings based on various consumer surveys and on ranking by accrediting groups, such as the National Committee for Quality Assurance (Washington, D.C.). The article concluded that "it is virtually impossible to make any sense of the assortment of rival and often contradictory systems for weeding out the good, the bad, and the ugly."[5] The main problem was the lack of comparability in the criteria used.

In an effort to quell the frequently heard criticism about clinical benchmarks being based on subjective assessments of providers or arbitrarily selected performance levels, researchers at the University of Alabama at Birmingham (UAB) have been examining a new methodology to create data-driven benchmarks that are objective and reproducible. The project, called Achievable Benchmarks of Care (ABC) was initiated in 1998 and is being conducted under a five-year grant from the Agency for Healthcare Research and Quality (AHRQ). Hopefully, the results of this research will help to identify hospitals that are truly "benchmarks" of excellence.

Finally, the Joint Commission on Accreditation of Healthcare Organizations (JCAHO) also hopes to provide some benchmark data for healthcare organizations by 2004.[6] A planned component of their "ORYX" initiative is the identification and use of core measures—standardized performance measures that can be applied across accredited healthcare organizations. Hospitals began collecting core measure data for patient discharges on July 1, 2002.

Benefits of Benchmarking

The above remarks are not meant to discourage healthcare providers from trying to contact other providers whom they feel are leaders in their field of interest. Thomas Pyzdek (1999) succinctly lists some benefits of competitive benchmarking in manufacturing that have application to healthcare as well[7]:

- Creating a culture that values continuous improvement to achieve excellence

- Enhancing creativity by devaluing the not-invented-here syndrome

- Increasing sensitivity to changes in the external environment

- Shifting the corporate mind-set from relative complacency to a strong sense of urgency for ongoing improvement

- Focusing resources through performance targets set with employee input

- Prioritizing the areas that need improvement

- Sharing the best practices between benchmarking partners

Pyzdek (1999) also warns that benchmarking can have dangers. Because benchmarking is based on learning from others, there may be a tendency to copy, rather than to develop new and improved ways of doing things. Therefore, it should never be the *primary* strategy for improvement.

SETTING GOALS AND TARGETS

After a team has finished selecting indicators for the process they hope to improve, the next questions they will ask are: "What are we trying to accomplish? How much do we hope to improve?" To answer these questions, it is often helpful to set a numerical target or goal. Setting numerical goals can be beneficial *when they are not set in an arbitrary fashion.*

Langley et al. (1996) make a good case in favor of setting numerical goals: "Numerical goals can be a convenient way to communicate expectations. Are small incremental improvements expected or are large breakthrough changes necessary? If the numerical goal is used well, it not only communicates the expectation, but also communicates the support that will be provided."[8]

However, setting *arbitrary* numerical goals will be counterproductive. Just giving a team a "stretch-goal" and letting them find out how to achieve it is not a sound idea. It is an abuse to hold people accountable for results they are incapable of achieving, or to give people a goal without a plan, method, and resources to meet it. The improvement team may be tempted to distort the data or meet the goal at the expense of others in the system.

Comparison Data

Finding comparison data from other providers can be useful for goal setting. Comparison data provide guidance to an organization on whether it should continue to monitor a process so as to maintain its current level of performance, or whether it should try to improve its current performance.

Comparison data can be obtained from a number of sources, such as the Joint Commission of Accreditation of Healthcare Organizations (Oakbrook Terrace, Illinois), the University Hospital Consortium (Oakbrook, Illinois), and the National Centers for Disease Control (Atlanta, Georgia). Data from these agencies should not be seen as providing exact numbers that are rigidly used for comparisons, because the information in their databases depends on the quality of data they receive from member organizations. These data are often of questionable accuracy. Nevertheless, these organizations can provide a reasonable estimate of what similar providers are doing. Using comparison data is different from benchmarking because the frame of reference is the experience of similar providers. There is no guarantee that the norm of general practice is one of excellence.

Lee and McGreevey (2002b) describe the Joint Commission's use of comparison charts in its accreditation surveys.[9] A comparison chart, a graphical summary of the comparison analysis, consists of actual (or observed) rates, expected rates, and expected ranges (upper and lower limits) for a given time frame. The charts tell an organization whether its performance is an "outlier" with respect to other similar organizations (using a 99 percent confidence level).

The JCAHO survey reports also provide control charts for the same indicators. Lee and McGreevey correctly emphasize that the control chart analysis is done *before* comparison analysis, to ensure the process stability. If a process is not stable, the observed performance data would not truly represent the performance capability of the organization. Comparisons would then be inappropriate.[10]

However, there are other ways of obtaining comparison data that can give a team an idea of what goals might be reasonable and attainable. Larger healthcare systems can examine data from member sites (hospitals, physician offices, long-term care facilities) to set reasonable goals. Local hospital councils and professional associations are also able to provide some comparative data that will help in goal setting.

Measuring Goal Achievement

Measuring whether or not a goal has been achieved presents an additional challenge. Using "t-tests" and other parametric statistics is usually not very helpful. One viable approach is to overlay the goal on a control chart after 20 or 25 points have been plotted and examine the stability of the process and its relationship to the goal. This approach will be demonstrated in chapter 8 where goals will be included on the control charts presented to a board of trustees.

In chapter 10, Dr. Larry Staker will illustrate two approaches to measuring goal achievement in the clinical care of *individual patients:* the percent treated-to-goal (TTG) and the six sigma statistic. The six sigma statistic will be discussed at length in chapter 9.

Exhibit 6.1   Indicator Development Form.

I. **Indicator identification**

1. What process are you trying to improve?

2. What is the name of the indicator?

3. What departments, services, or functions will be affected by this study?

4. What domain of quality does this indicator address?

   Clinical excellence (effectiveness)   _____

   Cost reduction (efficiency)   _____

   Patient satisfaction   _____

   Accreditation requirement   _____

   Safety requirement   _____

   Accessibility   _____

   Timeliness   _____

5. What is the source of this indicator?

   Journal reference: _____

   Other outside source:_____

   Developed internally by: _____

6. What is the operational definition of the indicator? (Be exact.)

---

continued

continued

II. Data collection plan

1. Who will be responsible for data collection?

2. How often will the data be collected?

3. For how long?

4. Sources for data? (for example, information system, finance office, physician's office, and so on)

5. Will sampling be used? If so, describe the sampling plan in detail.

III. Plan for analysis and reporting of results

1. Describe the plan for analysis.

2. What graphs will be used?

   Histogram   _____

   Pareto chart   _____

   Run chart   _____

   Control chart   _____   Which chart will you use? Why?

   Other   _____

3. Do you have baseline data for this indicator?

   If so, where did it come from? Describe it.

4. Is there a target or goal for this indicator?

   If so, where did it come from? Describe it.

5. Who will receive reports on the results? How often?

Exhibit 6.2 Sample indicators for a department of surgery

Surgical Division	Procedure	Indicator	Data Source
Thoracic/vascular	Lung resection	Chest tube > 5 days post-op	Hospital data system (HDS)
		Return to OR	HDS
		Return to ICU	HDS
		Death < 30 days	HDS
	Carotid endarterectomy	CVA < 30 days	Dr. office
		Readmit to hosp. < 30 days for same condition	HDS
		Mortality < 30 days	HDS
		Physician and nursing care scales	Patient survey
General surgery	Bowel resection	Return to OR	HDS
		Readmit < 30 days for same procedure	HDS
		Pulmonary embolism	HDS
		Deep vein thrombosis (DVT)	HDS
		Wound infection	HDS
		Post-op LOS	HDS
		Physician and nursing care scales	Patient survey
	Elective laparoscopic cholecysectomy	Readmit < 30 days	HDS
		Post-op LOS	HDS
Urology	TURP	Return to OR < 24 hours	HDS
		Fever > 101 within 48 hours	Patient chart
		Gross hematuria lasting 1 week after removal of catheter	Dr. office
Orthopedics	Total hip replacement	Pulmonary embolism < 45 days	Dr. office
		DVT < 45 days	Dr. office
		Dislocation < 45 days	Dr. office
		OR time	HDS
		Post-op LOS	HDS
Cardiac surgery	CABG	Mortality < 30 days of op	Dr. office
		Re-op for bleeding	HDS
		CVA < 30 days	Dr. office
		Post-op renal failure	HDS
		Prolonged (> 24 hrs.) ventilator usage	HDS
Ophthalmology	Mechanical vitrectomies	Questionable retinal detachment	Dr. office
		Rubeosis	Dr. office
		Cataract development	Dr. office
		Severe inflammation (Hypopyon)	Dr. office

continued

continued

Surgical Division	Procedure	Indicator	Data source
Plastic surgery	Breast reduction	Hematoma with return to OR < 48 hours.	Dr. office
		Nipple loss	Dr. office
	Breast reconstruction using tissue expander	Removal of implant <30 days	Dr. office
ENT	Tonsillectomy and/or adenoidectomy	Bleeding from mouth, nose, or vomiting fresh blood within 2 weeks	Dr. office
		Infection in fossa within 2 weeks	Dr. office
		Speech change < 3 weeks	Dr. office
Neurosurgery	Lumbar spinal fusion (non-instrument)	Recurrence of leg symptoms within 3 months	Dr. office
		Failure of fusion	Dr. office
		Wound infection within 3 weeks	HDS or Dr. office
	Ventriculoperitoneal shunt revision	Re-op < 30 days + CSF culture at time of VP shunt revision	HDS
Dental surgery	Any outpatient surgery	Unplanned emergent return to hosp. < 30 days for same surgery	HDS

ENDNOTES

1. For an illustration of a data gathering plan chart, I suggest consulting *Practical Tools for Continuous Improvement, Vol. 1,* Eds. J. D. Graham and M. J. Cleary (Miamisburg, OH: PQ Systems, 2000): 16–17.
2. R. Camp, *Benchmarking: The Search for Industry Best Practices That Lead to Superior Performance* (Milwaukee: ASQ Quality Press, 1989): 12.
3. Ibid., 15.
4. W. E. Deming, *The New Economics* (Boston: M.I.T. Center for Advanced Engineering Study, 1994): 36.
5. "The Ratings Game," *Wall Street Journal,* 19 October 1998.
6. K. Lee and C. McGreevey, "Using Comparison Charts to Assess Performance Measurement Data," *Journal on Quality Improvement* 28, no. 3 (March 2002): 129.
7. T. Pyzdek, *The Complete Guide to Six Sigma.* (Tucson, AZ: Quality Publishing, 1999): 222.
8. G. J. Langley, et al., *The Improvement Guide* (San Francisco: Jossey-Bass, 1996): 51.
9. Lee and McGreevey, "Using Comparison Charts to Assess Performance Measurement Data," 129–38.
10. Ibid., 131.

Part III

Special Applications of SPC Theory and Methods

7

Using Patient Feedback for Quality Improvement

This chapter has a narrow focus. It demonstrates how to apply the advanced SPC theory outlined in chapters 3, 4, and 5 to analyze patient survey data. The chapter is addressed both to those who administer surveys and to the end users of the survey results.

The subject of patient satisfaction surveys is very broad and requires an entire book to cover all the facets of this activity. Fortunately, an excellent text on the development and use of customer questionnaires has been written and should not only be read, but carefully studied, by those who have the responsibility of designing and/or implementing patient survey research. The book, *Measuring Customer Satisfaction* (1997), was written by Bob E. Hayes. His book covers the following issues not discussed in this chapter:

- Methods of determining the customer's quality dimensions that should be covered in a questionnaire

- The meaning and importance of the concepts of the validity and reliability of scales

- The characteristics of good questionnaire items and how to develop effective questions along with appropriate response formats

- The different uses of patient survey data, and how the intended use will govern the tools and types of analysis

- Examples of how control charts can be used to monitor customer satisfaction over time in non-healthcare settings

While Hayes does not have any specific examples relating to patient surveys, the theory he presents is directly applicable to obtaining and assessing patient feedback. His book describes complex questionnaire design issues and statistics in a way that is clear, concise, and understandable.

Another book that will be helpful to those in charge of implementing patient surveys in healthcare organizations is *The Practice of Social Research* (1998) by Earl Babbie. This book is much longer, more complex, and more academic than the book by Hayes. But Babbie addresses the important issues of sampling and adequate response rates not fully addressed by Hayes. Babbie also provides a more extensive treatment of questionnaire development and the issues of validity and reliability.

Readers of this book who have the responsibility of choosing an outside vendor to conduct their patient survey system may find my article, "How to Choose a Patient Survey System" (Carey 1999) of some assistance. Those interested in how to assess the validity and reliability of patient questionnaires will find this information in two other articles I co-authored, "A Patient Survey System to Measure Quality Improvement: Questionnaire Reliability and Validity" (Carey and Seibert 1993) and "Evaluating the Physician Office Visit: In Pursuit of a Valid and Reliable Measure of Quality Improvement Efforts" (Seibert, Strohmeyer, and Carey 1996).

Before presenting the two case studies in this chapter, I wish to highlight a few important distinctions.

PATIENT SATISFACTION VERSUS FUNCTIONAL ASSESSMENT

Feedback from patients regarding their satisfaction with the healthcare delivery process is not to be confused with patient feedback regarding their level of physical functioning. The so-called SF-36 and SF-12 functional self-assessment questionnaires developed by John Ware ask patients to evaluate themselves on various dimensions of physical and emotional well-being. These instruments are widely used in the United States and overseas by providers who wish to assess the *results* of medical care. They are particularly helpful in assessing the results of surgery on backs, hips, and knees, and on physical medical and rehabilitation patients who have suffered strokes or brain damage. They are less useful for patients receiving general medical treatment. I know of no other similar functional assessment instruments that have equal documentation of their validity and reliability.

The SF-36 and SF-12 questionnaires, when properly administered, are of value in assessing the long-term results of certain aspects of patient care. They are generally intended to be completed by patients three or four times: before surgery, and then at three months, six months, and a year afterwards. It is difficult to motivate most patients to fill out these questionnaires more than once or twice. Comparing groups of patients at different intervals becomes questionable with unequal response rates. Consequently, these data are not generally analyzed with control charts. These questionnaires are best used in basic research.

Patient feedback on the delivery of healthcare is different from feedback on functional assessment. It is also different than asking patients to evaluate the "quality of medical care." Patients are not ordinarily the best judge of the accuracy of a physician's diagnosis or the quality of a physician's technical skill. Indeed, it is possible for the "best possible care" to have poor results and for "poor" care to have good results. But the patient can provide valuable feedback on the *quality of the delivery process.* For example, patients can provide information on adequacy of pain management, or on whether or not they understood their diagnosis, treatment plan, and discharge instructions. They can say whether or not their family was kept properly informed, whether they felt they were treated with courtesy, and whether their privacy was respected. Their feelings may not always be objectively accurate, but their feelings are an objective reality that providers ought to address.

USES OF PATIENT SATISFACTION DATA

Data obtained from patient satisfaction surveys can have various uses. The tools used to analyze patient data will be determined by the intended use. Control charts are by no means the only tools to be employed. A few possible uses of data are described below.

Identifying Important Issues

Providers need to know which issues are most important to patient satisfaction. For inpatients, what are the relative importance of physician care, nursing care, and various "hotel" issues, such as housekeeping, food service, and so on? What are the most important factors influencing satisfaction with physician care? Nursing care? What are the critical issues for patients coming to the emergency department? To ambulatory care?

Identifying the relative value of various issues for various situations is best done by using correlational analysis (such as the Pearson Product Moment Correlation) relating patient satisfaction on specific issues with overall satisfaction. (The two articles I co-authored and cited above provide examples of this type of analysis.)

Measuring the Current Level of Satisfaction

To determine how well providers are addressing the key issues identified through correlational analysis, one can present the means and standard deviations of specific items, as well as overall scores for each dimension of importance. Descriptive statistics are "snapshots" of patient perceptions, but do not by themselves tell us whether a process is improving or deteriorating.

Assessing the Effect of Interventions

Control charts are the appropriate method of measuring process improvement over time in order to assess the effect of intervention. The specific type of chart will depend on whether you collected count data or measurement data. If you collected your data as count data, then you might use one of the attribute charts (P-, C-, or U-chart). If you collected measurement data (using a Likert scale of some kind), then you can use one of the variable charts (X-bar and S-chart, or an I-chart). The first case study below on nursing satisfaction will provide an example of a P-chart. The second case study on satisfaction with physician care in an ambulatory setting will illustrate variable charts.

Setting Goals

Analyzing patient data internally on the basis of hospital unit or office site can be useful for goal setting. Data from other similar facilities can also help determine what is realistically possible. However, comparisons should be made with other facilities that are using the *same survey instrument*. Attention should also be given to whether sampling methods and response rates are relatively equal and adequate.

QUALITATIVE VERSUS QUANTITATIVE DATA

Qualitative data are the type of data obtained through write-in comments on patient questionnaires or through focus groups. These data are sometimes useful for identifying potential areas for improvement, or for identifying issues that one wishes to address in a written questionnaire. However, it is not possible to generalize the findings of qualitative data to a larger population. It is very difficult, if not impossible, to measure the effect of an intervention using qualitative data.

Quantitative data are ordinarily obtained through a structured questionnaire—whether this is a person-to-person interview, a phone interview, or a written questionnaire. Each of these three methods of data collection has its own strengths and weaknesses. All three are subject to the possibility of bias. Person-to-person and telephone interviews have better response rates than written questionnaires, but tend to have "interviewer bias," that is, a positive response bias. Written questionnaires are less expensive and less open to a positive response bias, but tend to have lower response rates than phone or person-to-person interviews. Exactly what constitutes a "good" response rate is open to much debate. The subject is discussed at some length by Babbie (1998). He concludes that a "response rate of 50 percent is *adequate* for analysis and reporting. A response of 60 percent is *good*. And a response rate of 70 percent is *very good*."[1]

The first case study that follows is based on data from phone interviews. The second case study uses data from a written questionnaire.

CASE STUDY: IMPROVING NURSING CARE AMONG INPATIENTS

The Situation

Samaritan Hospital is part of a four hospital system. Samaritan wants to know whether inpatient satisfaction with nursing has been improving and how its nursing satisfaction compares to other hospitals in the system. All four hospitals conduct phone interviews using the same questionnaire. Each week for 20 consecutive weeks, Samaritan successfully contacted 60 patients: 30 patients from the medical unit, 20 from the surgical unit, and 10 from the OB unit. The nursing scale is composed of nine questions, each of which the patients rated as "excellent, very good, good, fair, or poor." The system had decided that the operational definition of "favorable response" would be a response of "excellent" to an item, and that an "unfavorable response" would be any of the other four categories.

Table 7.1 shows the results of the phone interviews for 20 consecutive weeks during 1999. Figure 7.1 is a P-chart analyzing the data aggregated for all three nursing units. The chart shows that 28.2 percent of all patients at Samaritan had one or more unfavorable responses. The P-chart also includes a comparison line (20 percent) which is the combined average of the other three hospitals.

Questions

1. Has overall nursing satisfaction improved over the last 20 weeks?

2. Is Samaritan a special cause with respect to the other hospitals?

3. What should Samaritan do next in analyzing the data?

Table 7.1 Patients with one or more "unfavorable" responses.

Week	All Pts.	1 or More Unfavorable Responses	Med. Pts.	1 or More Unfavorable Responses	Surg. Pts.	1 or More Unfavorable Responses	OB Pts.	1 or More Unfavorable Responses
1	60	17	30	4	20	12	10	1
2	60	13	30	6	20	6	10	1
3	60	15	30	5	20	11	10	2
4	60	15	30	4	20	8	10	3
5	60	16	30	7	20	9	10	0
6	60	16	30	3	20	12	10	1
7	60	23	30	7	20	13	10	3
8	60	18	30	4	20	13	10	1
9	60	19	30	6	20	11	10	2
10	60	18	30	9	20	9	10	0
11	60	16	30	7	20	7	10	2
12	60	18	30	3	20	14	10	1
13	60	12	30	2	20	9	10	1
14	60	17	30	9	20	6	10	2
15	60	13	30	8	20	5	10	0
16	60	14	30	5	20	7	10	2
17	60	17	30	6	20	10	10	1
18	60	17	30	4	20	12	10	1
19	60	25	30	7	20	14	10	3
20	60	20	30	5	20	13	10	2
Totals	1200	339	600	111	400	201	200	29

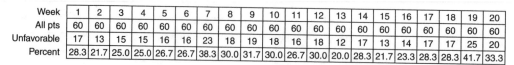

Week	1	2	3	4	5	6	7	8	9	10	11	12	13	14	15	16	17	18	19	20
All pts	60	60	60	60	60	60	60	60	60	60	60	60	60	60	60	60	60	60	60	60
Unfavorable	17	13	15	15	16	16	23	18	19	18	16	18	12	17	13	14	17	17	25	20
Percent	28.3	21.7	25.0	25.0	26.7	26.7	38.3	30.0	31.7	30.0	26.7	30.0	20.0	28.3	21.7	23.3	28.3	28.3	41.7	33.3

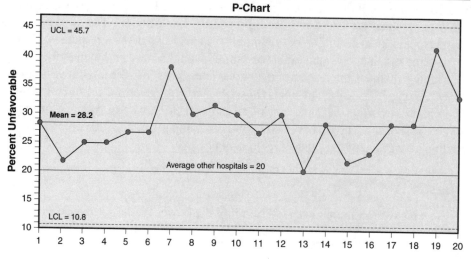

Figure 7.1   All patients in 1999—percent with one or more unfavorable responses.
Goal is to be under the average of other hospitals, for example, under 20 percent.

Analysis and Interpretation

1. There are no special causes. Week 19 (41 percent) is the highest of all weeks, but it is not above the UCL. The last eight weeks appear to show an "upward pattern." But this is not a trend, which requires six or seven consecutively increasing points. Therefore, the process is stable and predictable. If nothing is done to change the process, one can expect the average of unfavorable responses to be about 28 percent.

2. Yes, Samaritan is a special cause in comparison to the other hospitals: 19 or 20 weeks are above the average of the other hospitals. Therefore, while the process is stable and predictable, it is unacceptable.

3. If Samaritan wishes to improve, it should begin by disaggregating the data by organizational unit. Figure 7.2 displays the data from Table 7.1—rationally ordered by the three units: medical, surgical, and OB.

Questions

4. What did you learn from Figure 7.2? Are any of the units a special cause?

5. What should be done next?

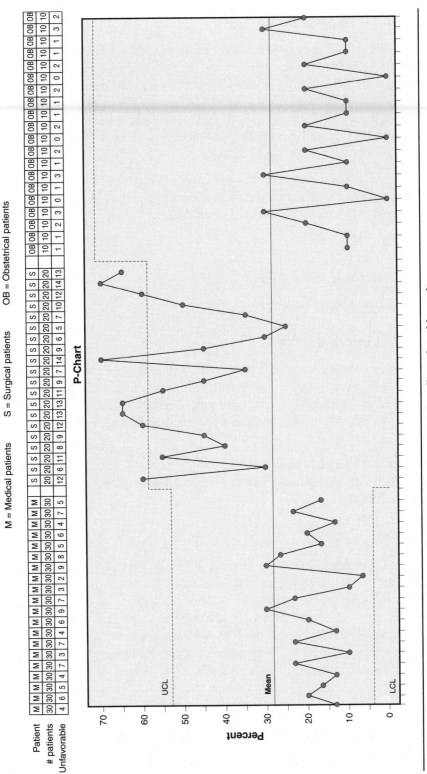

Figure 7.2   Percent with one or more unfavorable responses—rationally ordered by unit.

Analysis and Interpretation

4. In Figure 7.2 the mean is calculated *based on all 60 data points*. There are signals for special causes that indicate the three units are different. The medical and OB units are positive special causes, while the surgical unit is a negative special cause. Each unit has a run of eight or more weeks on one side of the mean (28 percent). In addition, the surgical unit has eight weeks above the UCL. Notice that the UCL varies in relation to the number of patients who responded for each unit.

5. The next step is to generate *separate control limits* for each unit to determine whether each unit is stable within itself and also to provide a baseline against which to measure future results (Figure 7.3).

Questions

6. What did you learn from Figure 7.3?

7. What should be the next step?

Analysis and Interpretation

6. All three units are stable and predictable within themselves, because they each have 20 consecutive points with only common cause variation. The medical unit with 18.5 percent unfavorable responses and the OB unit with 14.5 percent unfavorable responses are meeting the system goal of being under 20 percent.

7. The medical and OB units should continue to monitor their satisfaction to maintain their current levels of satisfaction. The surgical unit needs to develop an improvement plan

The Situation in 2000

The nurses on the surgical unit constructed a Pareto chart to see which items were scored most unfavorably by patients. It showed that only two of the nine items received almost all of the unfavorable responses: 1) failure to answer the call button promptly, and 2) failure to receive medications in a timely manner. The nurses developed an improvement plan in the last weeks of 1999 and then conducted a follow-up phone survey in the first months of 2000. The results are shown in Figure 7.4. Figure 7.5 shows the aggregated data comparing 1999 with 2000.

Questions

8. Was the improvement plan on the surgical unit a success?

9. Is Samaritan Hospital now meeting its goal of keeping the percent of patients with one or more unfavorable responses under 20 percent?

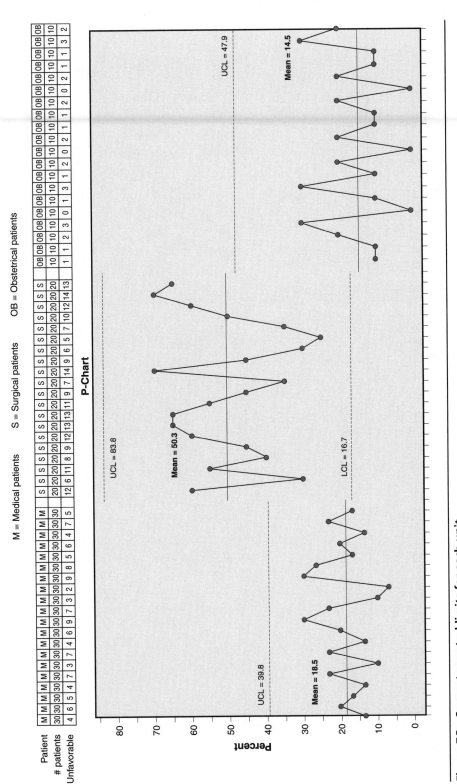

Figure 7.3 Separate control limits for each unit.

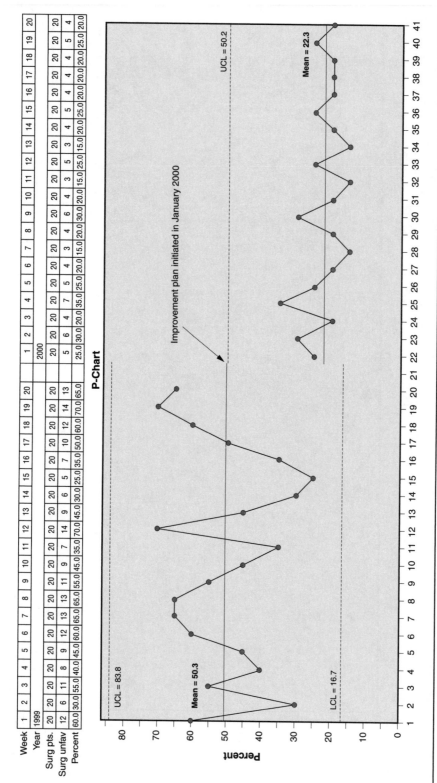

Week	1	2	3	4	5	6	7	8	9	10	11	12	13	14	15	16	17	18	19	20
Year	1999																			
Surg pts.	20	20	20	20	20	20	20	20	20	20	20	20	20	20	20	20	20	20	20	20
Surg unfav	12	6	11	8	9	12	13	13	11	9	7	14	9	6	5	7	10	12	14	13
Percent	60.0	30.0	55.0	40.0	45.0	60.0	65.0	65.0	55.0	45.0	35.0	70.0	45.0	30.0	25.0	35.0	50.0	60.0	70.0	65.0

Week	1	2	3	4	5	6	7	8	9	10	11	12	13	14	15	16	17	18	19	20
Year	2000																			
Surg pts.	20	20	20	20	20	20	20	20	20	20	20	20	20	20	20	20	20	20	20	20
Surg unfav	5	6	4	7	5	4	3	4	6	4	3	5	3	4	5	4	4	4	5	4
Percent	25.0	30.0	20.0	35.0	25.0	20.0	15.0	20.0	30.0	20.0	15.0	25.0	15.0	20.0	25.0	20.0	20.0	20.0	25.0	20.0

P-Chart

Improvement plan initiated in January 2000

UCL = 50.2
Mean = 22.3

UCL = 83.8
Mean = 50.3
LCL = 16.7

Percent

Figure 7.4   Surgical unit—percent unfavorable before and after improvement plan (historical chart).

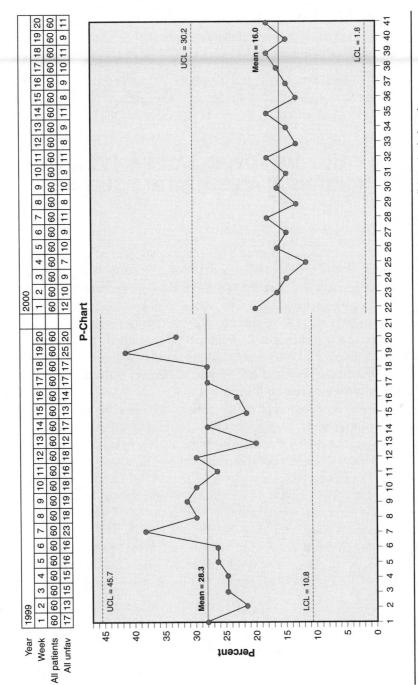

Year	1999																				2000																				
Week	1	2	3	4	5	6	7	8	9	10	11	12	13	14	15	16	17	18	19	20	1	2	3	4	5	6	7	8	9	10	11	12	13	14	15	16	17	18	19	20
All patients	60	60	60	60	60	60	60	60	60	60	60	60	60	60	60	60	60	60	60	60	60	60	60	60	60	60	60	60	60	60	60	60	60	60	60	60	60	60	60	60
All unfav	17	13	15	15	16	16	23	18	19	18	16	18	12	17	13	14	17	25	20		12	10	9	7	10	9	11	8	10	9	11	8	9	11	8	9	10	11	9	11

Figure 7.5 All patients: 1999–2000—percent with one or more "unfavorable" responses (historical chart).

Analysis and Interpretation

8. The surgical unit's level of satisfaction is clearly a special cause with relation to its 1999 process. All 20 weeks are below the 1999 baseline (50.3 percent). Its 2000 process is stable and predictable with only 22.3 percent of patients with an unfavorable response.

9. While the surgical unit is still slightly above 20 percent unfavorable (Figure 7.4), Samaritan's aggregated score for the three units in 2000 is not only better than the 1999 mean (28 percent), but is clearly under the 20 percent target.

CASE STUDY: IMPROVING SATISFACTION WITH PHYSICIANS IN AN OUTPATIENT SETTING

The Situation

A Midwestern healthcare system operated several outpatient care sites, each with three specialties: Family Practice (FP), Pediatrics (Peds), and Ambulatory Surgery (Surg). The system leadership decided that the results of the patient satisfaction survey conducted by the corporate quality department would be one of the factors in determining physician compensation. To insure that the survey results would be based on high quality data, the system had chosen a physician office visit survey that had good validity and reliability (Seibert, et al. 1996), employed the same sampling procedure at all sites, and consistently obtained a response rate of over 50 percent. All data were collected by means of a mailed survey to reduce interviewer bias.

The various sites were compared on the basis of the questionnaire's physician care scale which was composed of 10 questions. Patients rated each question as: "excellent, very good, good, fair, or poor." The answers were scored from five (excellent) to one (poor) and the average of the 10 questions determined the physician care scale score. Physicians at all the sites agreed that an annual site score of 4.0 or better ("very good") would be required for physicians at a given site to get the annual bonus.

Data were collected and analyzed monthly during the year 1999. Figure 7.6 presents an X-bar and S-control chart analyzing the data for Site A. The physicians at Site A were disappointed to find that the average score for all three departments taken together for 1999 was 3.83, which meant they would not receive their bonuses for that year. The average of all other sites was 4.1, suggesting that improvement was possible at Site A.

Questions

1. Why did the physicians choose an X-bar and S-chart?

2. What did the physicians learn from the X-bar and S-chart?

3. What is their next step if they wish to improve?

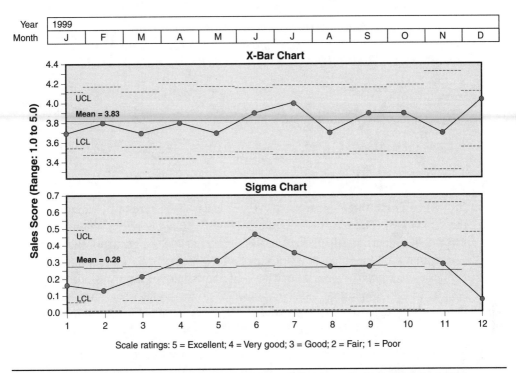

Figure 7.6   **Average physician care scale at Site A, all three services combined—1999.**
Average of all other sites in healthcare system = 4.1.

Analysis and Interpretation

1. A scale score (that is, the average of several items) is measurement data and therefore the choice of control chart is between an X-bar and S-chart and an I-chart. Because each subgroup ("month" in this case) has more than one measurement (that is, more than one patient), the better choice is an X-bar and S-chart. The S-chart will show whether there was a special cause within each subgroup. The X-chart will show whether the process has changed over time. Plotting the average monthly scale score on an I-chart would not tell us whether or not there was an unusual amount of variation within any month.

2. There were only 12 points on the chart in Figure 7.6. It would be better to have 20 points to be certain of the stability of the process. However, based on the available data, which produced "trial limits," the process seems to be stable. However, the process is unacceptable because the mean (3.83) is less than 4.0, which would be equivalent to an overall "very good" rating. Improvement is clearly possible because the other sites are averaging 4.1. Notice that the run of eight points *above* the mean of the *sigma* chart suggests that there may be wide variation among physicians during those months.

3. The next step is to stratify the data by organizational unit (Family Practice, Pediatrics, and Ambulatory Surgery), rationally ordering the data on the same control chart (Figure 7.7).

Questions

4. What did you learn from Figure 7.7?

5. What is the next step?

Analysis and Interpretation

4. In Figure 7.7 the three departments (service areas) are rationally ordered on the same chart. The mean is computed from all 36 data points. When the three departments are displayed on the same chart, it is clear from the special causes that the three areas are not viewed the same way by the patients. Pediatrics is a *positive* special cause, while ambulatory surgery is a *negative* special cause. Notice that the special causes on the sigma chart suggests that there is *little* variation among pediatricians (smaller standard deviations), but *considerable* variation between surgeons (larger standard deviations).

5. The next step is to develop *separate* control limits for each area (Figure 7.8) to see whether each of their processes is stable and to establish a baseline for future improvement efforts.

Questions

6. What do you learn from Figure 7.8?

7. What should be the next steps?

Analysis and Interpretation

6. Figure 7.8 shows that based on trial limits, all three areas are stable. The mean for two areas are below the 4.0 average needed for obtaining bonuses. Family Practice has a mean of 3.87 and Surgery a mean of 3.33. In addition, the S-chart for Surgery shows a special cause with eight consecutive points above the its mean. This means that there is more *variability* in patient responses than in the Family Practice and Pediatric service areas. Because there are only two surgeons at this site, this variability suggests that the two surgeons might be viewed quite differently by patients.

7. Both Family Practice and Surgery need to develop improvement plans, while Pediatrics needs to maintain its positive patient ratings. Family Practice and Surgery need to investigate the 10 items making up the Physician Scale and find out where they should concentrate their efforts. A Pareto chart will be a useful tool to identify these items. Based on the findings in the S-chart, Surgery might find it helpful to plot the scale scores for its two surgeons on the same chart.

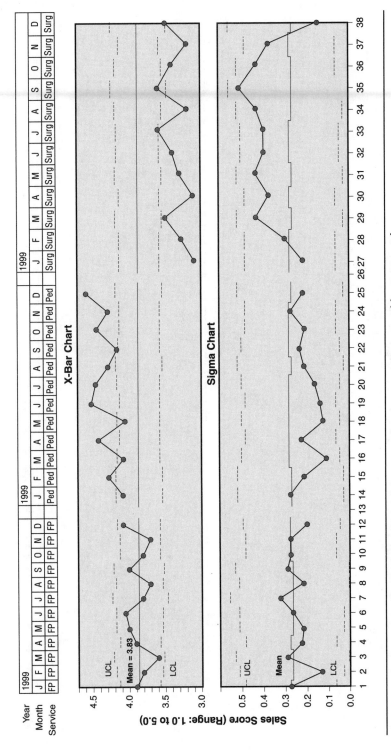

Figure 7.7   Rational ordering of physician scale scores for three service areas (departments).

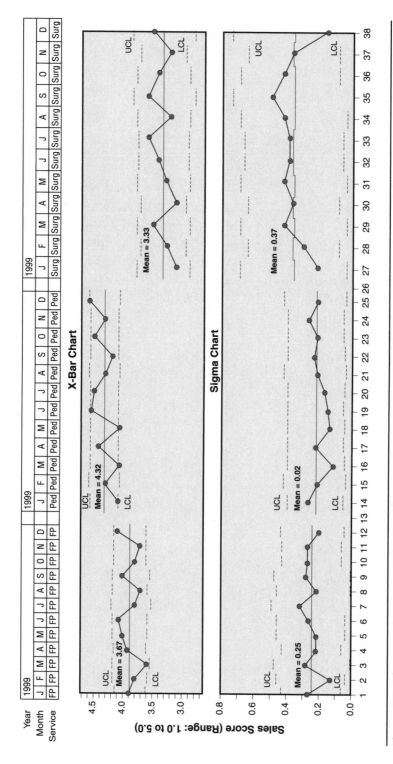

Figure 7.8   Three service areas at Site A with separate control limits.

The Situation in 2000

In January 2000, Surgery plotted the ratings *from 20 consecutive patients* for each of its two surgeons on an I-chart (Figure 7.9). Next, Pareto charts were developed for Surgery and Family Practice items from 1999. The surgeons found that they received their lowest ratings on: "the physician's personal manner" and "questions answered after the visit." Family Practice received its lowest ratings in 1999 on two items: "time spent with the physician" and "explanation of diagnosis and treatment." Physicians in both areas discussed these issues and planned how they might be more sensitive to patients' feelings. They then collected additional data for the 12 months in 2000 and compared their scores to 1999. Figure 7.10 shows the findings for Surgery, and Figure 7.11 for Family Practice.

Questions

8. Why did the surgeons use an *I-chart* (Figure 7.9) to analyze the ratings from 20 consecutive patients on Surgeon M and Surgeon J collected in January 2000? What do you learn by rationally ordering ratings of the two surgeons on the same chart?

9. Was the Surgery Department's improvement plan introduced in January 2000 effective (Figure 7.10)?

10. Was the Family Practice improvement plan introduced in January 2000 effective (Figure 7.11)?

Analysis and Interpretation

8. The surgeons used an I-chart, not an X-bar and S-chart, in January 2000 because the "subgroups" were 20 *individual patients,* not 20 *groups* of respondents. This enabled them to move quickly to diagnosis their difficulties. Surgeon M was clearly seen by patients more positively than Surgeon J. However, both were improving with patients seen later in the month of January, as is evidenced by the special causes in Figure 7.9. Surgeon M had a run of seven points over the mean, while Surgeon J's last patient rating was over the UCL. Their discussion of the ways to improve patient interaction shows signs of being productive.

9. Figure 7.10 shows that the improvement plan was effective in the surgical service area. All 12 months of 2000 were above the 1999 mean (3.33)! Surgery's ratings for 2000 were now averaging 4.03—over the target of 4.0.

Surgeon	M	M	M	M	M	M	M	M	M	M	M	M	M	M	M	M	M	M	M	M
Patient	1	2	3	4	5	6	7	8	9	10	11	12	13	14	15	16	17	18	19	20
	3.2	3.4	3.6	3.3	3.3	3.3	3.4	3.8	3.7	3.8	3.5	3.5	3.7	4.0	4.2	3.9	3.9	3.7	4.0	3.9

Surgeon	J	J	J	J	J	J	J	J	J	J	J	J	J	J	J	J	J	J	J	J
Patient	1	2	3	4	5	6	7	8	9	10	11	12	13	14	15	16	17	18	19	20
	3.2	3.1	2.9	2.8	2.7	3.0	3.1	3.0	3.0	3.1	2.9	2.8	2.7	2.6	2.9	3.1	3.0	3.1	3.2	3.4

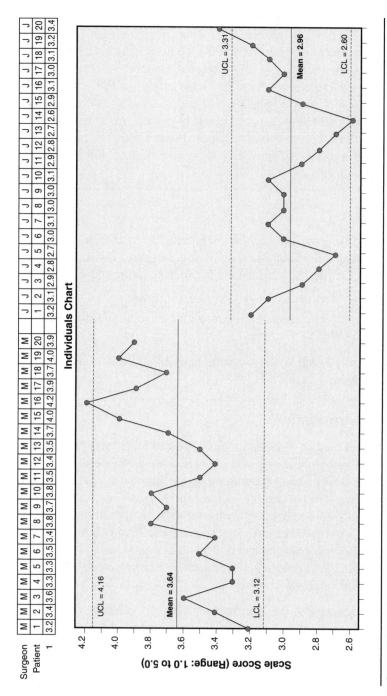

Individuals Chart

UCL = 4.16
Mean = 3.64
LCL = 3.12

UCL = 3.31
Mean = 2.96
LCL = 2.60

Scale Score (Range: 1.0 to 5.0)

4.2
4.0
3.8
3.6
3.4
3.2
3.0
2.8
2.6

Figure 7.9 Rational ordering of physician scale scores for two surgeons: M and J.
Ratings are from 20 consecutive patients for each surgeon in January 2000.

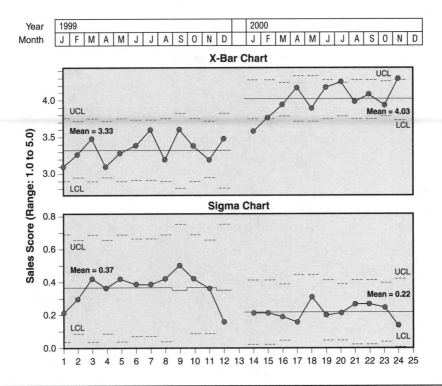

Figure 7.10   Surgical patient ratings before and after intervention in January 2000.

10. Figure 7.11 shows that the improvement efforts of Family Practice were ineffective. The 1999 mean (3.87) was extended at the time of the intervention in January 2000. The run of four months at the beginning of 2000 is not long enough to be a special cause. The ratings for 2000 continue to revolve around the 1999 mean, showing common cause variation. The physicians must now investigate the reason for the ineffectiveness of their intervention. Was it because their plan was conceptually unsound? Or was it because the plan was not properly implemented? After discussing possible answers to these questions, the physicians should then introduce a new improvement effort and plot data from the year 2001 using the 24 months of 1999–2000 as a baseline. This trial and error procedure is an example of the plan–do–study–act cycle.

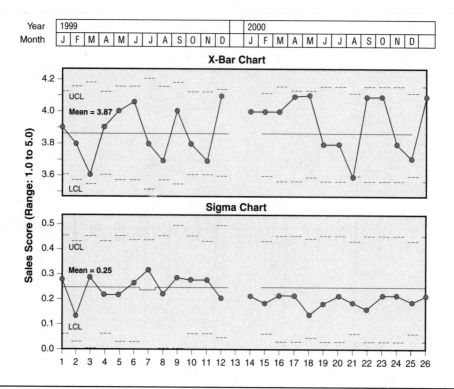

Figure 7.11   Family practice patient ratings before and after intervention in January 2000.
Mean is extended at the time of the intervention in January 2000.

ENDNOTE

1. E. Babbie, *The Practice of Social Research*, 8th ed. (New York: Wadsworth Publishing Company, 1998): 262.

8

Governance and Monitoring Quality

T he subject of the role of governance in healthcare is wide-ranging and complicated. After attending a number of presentations on the role and function of
trustees sponsored by the American College of Healthcare Executives (Chicago,
Illinois) and the Institute of Healthcare Improvement (Boston, Massachusetts), I found
myself overwhelmed by the complexity of the issues and conflicting advice.

Therefore, this chapter will not attempt to address all the aspects of governance,
which are best covered in an entire book dedicated to the subject. Instead, it is my
intention to focus on one facet of the role of governance, namely, its responsibility to
oversee the quality of care offered by a healthcare provider. Furthermore, no attempt
is made to settle into all the theoretical disputes that can be raised in this area. Instead,
I have chosen a more pragmatic approach. I would like to share some suggestions
based on personal experience that may be of assistance to those who serve on boards
of directors or who prepare material for presentation to boards. In particular, the focus
will be on how trustees can be more statistically sophisticated in analyzing data on the
quality of care through the use of control charts, "balanced scorecards," goal setting,
and comparison data.

I have been privileged to have had positive experiences in oversight roles. First, I
spent 20 years as a voting member of a quality oversight committee at a large teaching
hospital that prepared data for submission to a board of trustees. I also served for three
years on the "Medical/Clinical Affairs Committee" of the board of a large healthcare
system where I reviewed data submitted by physicians and other providers. During both
experiences, I was honored to work alongside of physicians, nurses, and lay board
members who were not only dedicated to improving quality, but who were reasonably
successful in their efforts. They were effective in their oversight responsibilities because
they were flexible and open to change, continually engaging in self-evaluation and self-
criticism. I am indebted to them for the thoughts and suggestions that are offered in this

chapter. Yet, these ideas are offered with the realization that what works in one situation may not work in another.

This chapter is divided into the following topics:

- Organizational structure

- Role of governance with respect to quality

- Developing a balanced scorecard

- Displaying and reviewing scorecard data

ORGANIZATIONAL STRUCTURE

It is difficult to outline an organizational structure that will facilitate a board's ability to effectively monitor quality without knowing something about the organization. The structure will differ by type of healthcare organization (hospital, long-term care facility, nursing home, and so on), by the size of the organization (a small community hospital, a large healthcare system), and by the extent of the services provided.

In the case of a free-standing hospital, an oversight committee of the medical staff (often called the "Quality Assurance Committee" or "Quality Improvement Committee") may assume the role of monitoring quality of care and reporting directly to the Board of Trustees. In the case of a multi-hospital system, the Board will often create a subcommittee to review medical and clinical issues. This subcommittee meets prior to each meeting of the full board and presents a summary of its findings to the entire board.

How should membership on such a "medical/clinical affairs" subcommittee be determined? The mistake I observed was allowing each major organizational unit in the system to have its own representative. The committee became very large (over 25 members). Some members were mainly interested in assuring that nothing "damaging" was said about their areas but lacked the commitment to promote quality improvement throughout the system. The length of the meetings (two hours) did not allow for meaningful discussion by all present. The result was poor attendance, as well as members coming late to the meetings or leaving early.

I found that a quality subcommittee functioned more effectively when membership was relatively small (no more than 10 members)—and was composed mainly of physicians and nurses with perhaps an "outside expert" in data analysis. Members were not there as "representatives" of a provider group, but were committed to impartially assessing quality throughout the entire system. They were expected to attend every meeting in person. Substitutes were not allowed, even in the case of unavoidable absences. Every member was expected to become statistically "literate" in the interpretation of data. Training courses and reading material on SPC tools were made available to the subcommittee members. The subcommittee met every two months and reviewed data organized and presented by senior leadership of the system (executive vice president of medical affairs and his/her staff). A summary report of each meeting was presented to the full board of trustees the following week.

ROLE OF GOVERNANCE WITH RESPECT TO QUALITY

The general purpose of an oversight committee on quality can be achieved by the following activities:

- Overseeing clinical quality measurement and outcomes

- Monitoring initiatives designed to improve the processes that drive patient satisfaction

- Identifying and sharing best practices

This purpose sounds reasonable and straightforward. But all the members may not agree on precisely what these activities entail. The committee I served on found it helpful to have all the members fill out a questionnaire at the beginning of each year that asked the members to identify and prioritize the committee's specific goals for the coming year. This was especially important, not only because there was some turnover in membership, but because priorities were constantly changing in response to changes in the healthcare environment and suspected problems within the system itself.

At the end of the year, our subcommittee assessed its performance on how well it achieved its stated goals from the previous year. We also routinely reviewed our quality improvement program using some general principles that stayed the same from year to year:

- Were our quality improvement efforts truly *systemwide*?

- Were the *physicians* involved in a significant and meaningful way?

- Were our improvement efforts focused on improving *systems*, not on the performance of individuals?

- What *specific steps* can leadership or governance take to improve quality that are not already being taken?

At each meeting, standing agenda items (that is, reviewing quality indicators and care management, patient satisfaction) provide the opportunity to discuss the structures and processes throughout the system that produce outcomes. Guests were invited periodically to provide updates on topics such as JCAHO accreditation and indicators, patient rights and responsibilities, and on research and education initiatives. The main document that was regularly presented and studied was the clinical scorecard (dashboard), which included patient satisfaction results (see below).

CONDUCTING PRODUCTIVE MEETINGS

Nothing can destroy the enthusiasm of committee members as much as frustration—a feeling that their time is not used well and that nothing is being accomplished to improve quality. Nothing will energize a committee more than meetings that are well-organized, well-chaired, and sharply focused on a meaningful agenda. A few suggestions might be useful:

1. *Maintain an attitude that care can and should be continually improved.* I remember hearing a quotation from Daniel Boorstin, the former head of the Library of Congress, that went something to the effect that: "The great obstacle to progress is not ignorance, but the illusion of knowledge." If there is any danger that board members must guard against it is being lulled to sleep by their system's reputation for excellence. Much of the "data" we use to support our claims of "quality care" are really anecdotal in nature. The board should continually challenge its own institution to present *data* to document its claims of excellence. The plural of "anecdote" is "anecdotes"—not data! The board has the difficult task of collecting and examining data dispassionately to determine: "Where are our areas of excellence? Where can we improve? How safe is the care we are giving our patients?" Board members must constantly remind themselves that obtaining accreditation from a regulatory body can never be equated with excellence.

2. *Carefully plan the agenda.* All presenters should speak to the committee chairperson before the meeting and agree on the amount of time needed for the presentation. The agenda with appropriate materials should be sent to the members before the meeting. The board is expected to come properly prepared. At the meeting itself, presenters should briefly summarize the subject matter and leave the majority of the allotted time for questions and discussion. The last-minute distribution of handouts is to be discouraged. Last-minute handouts suggest that the presenter is not properly prepared and prevent the committee from coming adequately prepared to discuss the material. The length of a meeting should ordinarily be limited to two hours. Meetings every two months are suggested, although quarterly meetings may be sufficient for smaller hospitals and long-term care facilities.

3. *Have strong committee leadership.* Committee members will be grateful for a chairperson who runs a meeting in a firm, but courteous manner. The leader should begin and end the meeting on time. If the two hours allotted for the meeting finds the committee in a crucial discussion, the chair should poll the members to see whether they will agree to allow the meeting to run overtime. During the meeting itself, the chair should make presenters stay within the time allotted—unless once again a vote of the committee allows a change in the scheduled time. This rule also applies to individuals with "status" in the system.

4. *Possess the essential statistical skills.* The critical criterion for committee membership is not that a person be well known and respected for his/her skills as a physician, nurse, or therapist. A desire to improve the current processes throughout

the system—along with data analytical skills—is more important. By data analytical skills, I refer not to the statistics required for basic research (such as the t-test, analysis of variance, Pearson product moment correlation, and so on), but to those SPC tools required to study and assess process improvement (such as Pareto charts, scatter diagrams, histograms, run charts, and control charts).

Unless members understand the need to look at data in a time-series design, they won't be able to recognize the difference between random data variation and a true change in a process. They also need to know how to interpret comparison data and to evaluate goal attainment.

DEVELOPING A BALANCED SCORECARD

Concepts

Kaplan and Norton (1996) claim to have introduced the concept of a "balanced scorecard."[1] The purpose of the scorecard in their view was to supplement "traditional financial measures with criteria that measured performance from three additional perspectives—those of customers, internal business processes, and learning and growth." The scorecard was intended to "link a company's long-term strategy with its short-term goals." Chow et al. (1998) picked up on the idea of a balanced scorecard from Kaplan and Norton and applied it to healthcare.[2] They offered some general guidance to healthcare organizations who wanted to develop indicators for their scorecards. They said the list of indicators should include not only outcome measures, but performance measures. Because outcome measures are not always sufficiently timely to alert remedial action, "performance drivers" also need to be included to serve as leading indicators of outcomes. The number of measures should be kept low so as not to dilute attention from key measures. They also supported the view of Kaplan and Norton that the measures should focus on strategic goals (for example, increasing healthcare quality), not on "diagnostic measures" (for example, improving cash flow).

The expression "dashboard" is often used in place of "balanced scorecard." It has taken various forms when implemented by the leadership and trustees of healthcare organizations. The concept of "quality compass" is another format that was developed from the balanced scorecard idea. The quality compass encouraged the development of indicators under four headings: financial, clinical, patient satisfaction (with the process of delivery of care), and functional outcomes (physical and emotional outcomes of care).

Development Guidelines

Robin Lawton (2002) offered some specific suggestions and guidelines for the development of indicators.[3] While Lawton writes principally for manufacturing organizations, most of the suggestions are adaptable to healthcare as well. As Lawton sees it, the balanced scorecard is a management decision tool to link strategy with operational performance measures. The indicators are meant to numerically define the meaning of success. Lawton suggests that the number of indicators should be limited to 20—all connected to strategic objectives. There should be some outcome and some process measures—all aligned with customer priorities or the organization's strategic objectives. Some should measure the desired and undesired outcomes, as well as the desired process characteristics of the customer. Other indicators should measure the outcomes and process characteristics desired by the organization. Only a few indicators should be kept forever. Most will change as strategic objectives and the environment change.

Let's apply these concepts and suggestions to a hospital system and list a few sample indicators for a typical dashboard. (See Exhibit 8.1.) Indicators are often grouped into one of three categories:

- Financial (operational) indicators, which are changed infrequently

- Clinical indicators (chosen from high volume or high risk processes, or suspected problem areas), which are changed as strategic objectives change

- Patient satisfaction indicators

The full board would review all indicators. The quality subcommittee would focus on clinical and patient satisfaction indicators and review them in depth.

Exhibit 8.1   Sample set of financial, clinical, and patient satisfaction indicators.

Indicator #	Indicator Category	Indicator	Focus
1	Financial	Net operating margin (NOM)	Outcome
2		Gross revenue	Outcome
3		Realization rate (% of gross revenue actually collected)	Outcome
4		Number of inpatient admissions	Process
5		Psychiatric inpatient market share	Process
6	Clinical	Acute myocardial infarction (AMI) mortality (Patients > 65)	Outcome
7		CABG mortality	Outcome
8		Perinatal and neonatal mortality	Outcome
9		Psychiatric readmissions < 30 days	Process
10		Congestive heart failure (CHF) readmission rate	Process
11		Time between positive mammogram and definitive biopsy	Process
12		Medication errors	Safety
13	Patient Satisfaction	Inpatient satisfaction	Outcome
14		ED patient satisfaction	Outcome
15		Outpatient surgery satisfaction	Outcome

DISPLAYING AND REVIEWING SCORECARD DATA

Let's examine two ways of displaying scorecard data: first, in table format and then through the use of control charts. The key learning point I wish to make is that summarizing dashboard data in tabular format has some value, but usually is not sufficient to allow the board to evaluate process improvement and goal attainment. Tabular format has the virtue of being concise and easy to read. But unless the process is stable and predictable, that is, has only common cause variation, the mean (average) score of the current period (whether it be month, quarter, or year) does not provide a true picture of the process. Nor can the mean of an unstable process be validly compared to a target or goal.

Look at the financial, clinical, and patient satisfaction indicators in the tabular format below, and see whether you can answer the following nine questions. And then when you have finished reviewing the tabular format, ask the same questions as you look at the data analyzed in the control chart format that follows. Which format do you find more helpful?

1. Did the net operating margin improve after the new CEO arrived in January 1999? (Figure 8.1)

2. What effect did the increase in room charges in April 1999 have on revenue and realization rate? (Figures 8.2 and 8.3)

3. What effect did the withdrawal of a large company from our health plan in November 1998 have on admissions? (Figure 8.4)

4. What effect did the opening of a competing psychiatric program in November 1998 have on market share? (Figure 8.5)

5. Have the mortality rates decreased for AMI patients (Figure 8.6), CABG surgery (Figure 8.7), and neonatal patients (Figure 8.8)?

6. Have readmission rates decreased for psychiatric patients (Figure 8.9) and CHF patients (Figure 8.10)?

7. Was the effort to decrease the delays between a positive mammogram and a definitive biopsy successful? (Figure 8.11)

8. How successful was the plan to decrease medication errors? (Figure 8.12)

9. Has patient satisfaction improved during 1999? (Figures 8.13, 8.14, and 8.15)

10. Which 1999 goals were met? (See all figures.)

Dashboard Displayed in Tabular Format

For an example of a dashboard in tabular format, see Exhibit 8.2.

Exhibit 8.2   Sample dashboard for board of trustees.

Indicator ID #	Indicator Category	Indicator	1998–1999 Average Score	1999 Goal	2000 Goal
1	Financial	Net operating margin (NOM)	7.53%	8%	9%
2		Gross revenue (in millions)	$38.34	$40	$41
3		Realization rate (% of gross revenue actually collected)	69.64%	68%	72%
4		Number of inpatient admissions	2102	2150	2200
5		Psychiatric inpatient market share	17.2%	18%	20%
6	Clinical	AMI mortality (Patients > 65)	9.67%	< 11%	< 9%
7		CABG mortality	5.46%	< 4%	< 2%
8		Perinatal and neonatal mortality	10.2 per 1000	< 11/1000	< 9/1000
9		Psychiatric readmissions < 30 days	9.25%	< 8%	< 8%
10		CHF readmission rate	12.7 %	< 10%	< 8%
11		Delay between positive mammogram and biopsy	25.67 days	< 24 days	< 20 days
12		Medication errors	5.5 per 1000	< 6/1000	<5/1000
13	Patient Satisfaction	Inpatient satisfaction	83%	> 85%	> 90%
14		ED patient satisfaction	72.5%	> 75%	> 80%
15		Outpatient surgery satisfaction	78.17%	> 75%	> 80%

Dashboard Displayed in Control Chart Format

Financial indicators are net operating margin (Figure 8.1); gross revenue (Figure 8.2); realization rate (Figure 8.3); inpatient admissions (Figure 8.4); and psychiatric patient market share (Figure 8.5).

Clinical indicators are AMI mortality rate of patients > 65 (Figure 8.6); CABG mortality (Figure 8.7); perinatal and neonatal mortality (Figure 8.8); psychiatric readmissions < 30 days (Figure 8.9); CHF readmission rate (Figure 8.10); time between positive mammogram and definitive biopsy (Figure 8.11); and medication errors (Figure 8.12).

Patient satisfaction indicators are Inpatient (Figure 8.13); Emergency Department (Figure 8.14); and Outpatient Surgery (Figure 8.15).

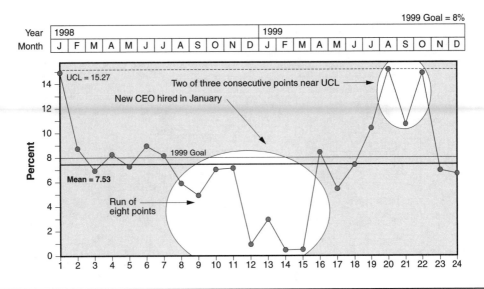

Figure 8.1 Net operating margin.

Two special causes—NOM improves after new CEO hired in January 1999.

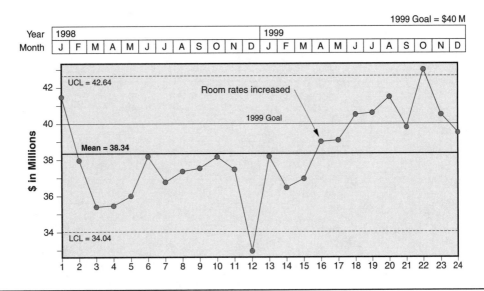

Figure 8.2 Gross revenue (in millions).

1999 is a positive special cause.

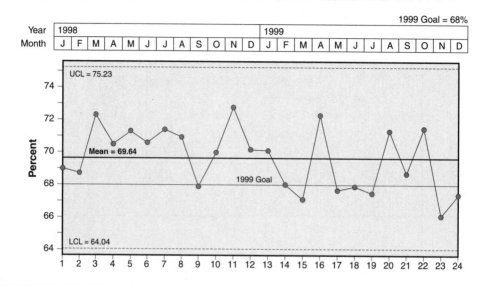

Figure 8.3   Realization rate.

Realization rate = 1 – (Total deductions from revenue + bad debt expense/total patient revenue).

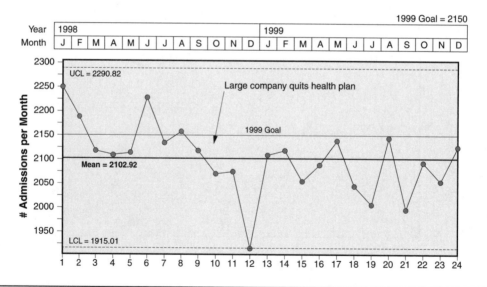

Figure 8.4   Inpatient admissions.

1998 is a special cause, number of admissions decreased in 1999.

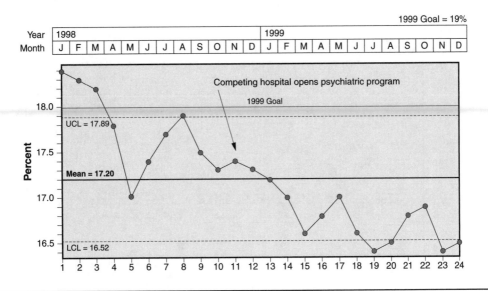

Figure 8.5   Psychiatric inpatient market share.

1999 is a special cause, signaling sharp decrease in market share.

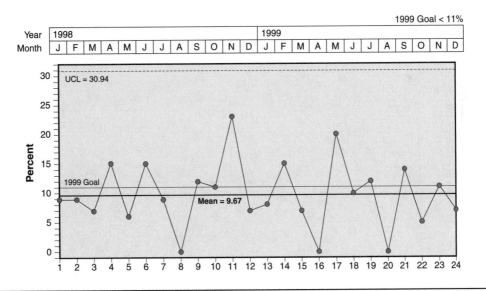

Figure 8.6   AMI mortality (patients 65 and older).

Common cause variation, rate is stable and predictable.

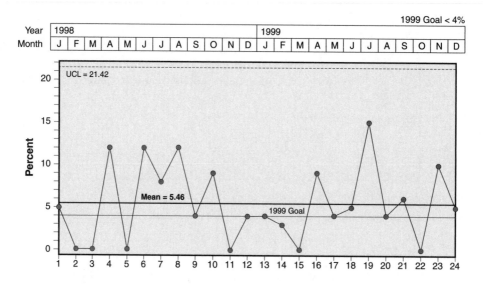

Figure 8.7 Coronary artery bypass graft (CABG) mortality.
Common cause variation, rate is stable and predictable.

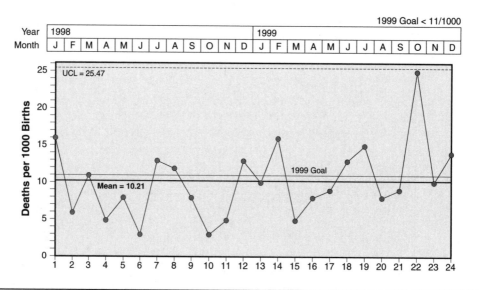

Figure 8.8 Perinatal and neonatal mortality (deaths/1000 births).
Rate is stable and predictable at 10.2 deaths per 1000.

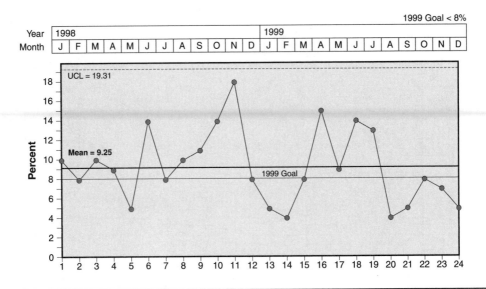

Figure 8.9   Psychiatric readmissions within 30 days.

Rate is stable and predictable at 9.2% readmissions per month.

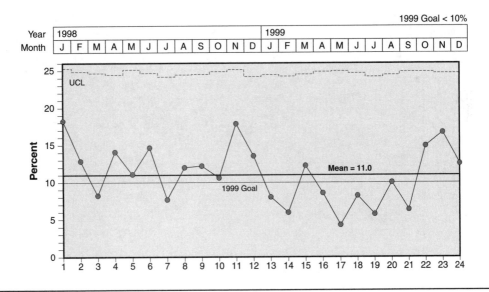

Figure 8.10   CHF readmission rate.

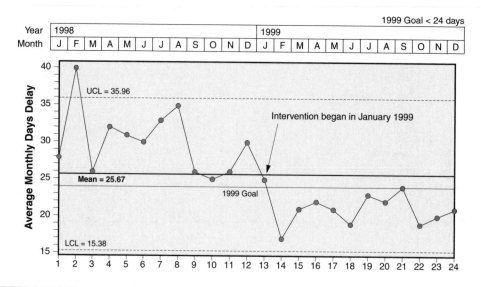

Figure 8.11 Delay between positive mammogram and biopsy.
Special cause in 1999 signals success of intervention.

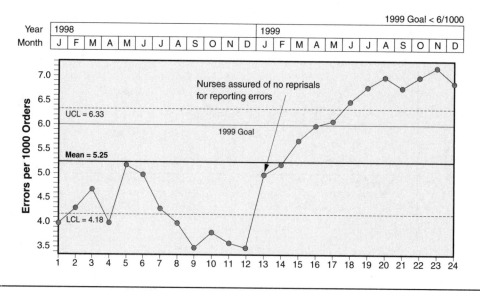

Figure 8.12 Medication errors (errors per 1000 orders).
1999 is a special cause signaling sharp increase in error rate.

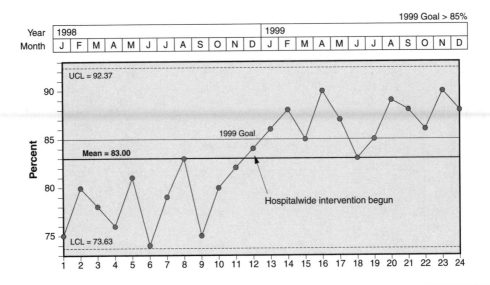

Figure 8.13   Inpatient satisfaction.
Percent likely to recommend hospital to family and friends. 1999 is a special cause signaling success of intervention.

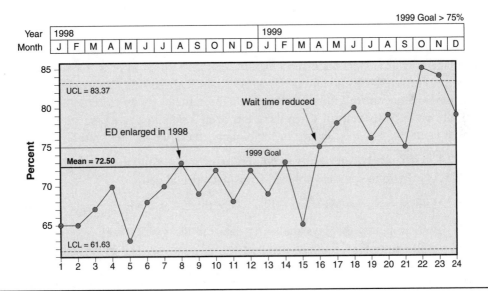

Figure 8.14   Emergency department patient satisfaction.
Percent "likely to recommend ED to family and friends." 1999 is a special cause signaling the success of intervention.

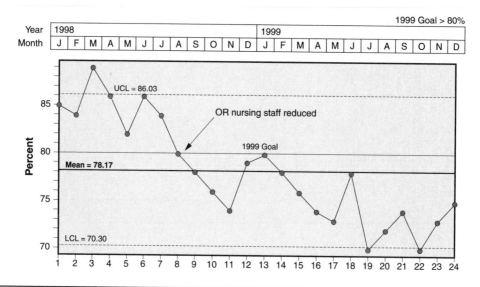

Figure 8.15   Outpatient surgery patient satisfaction.

Percent likely to "recommend to family and friends." 1999 is a special cause signaling deteriorating patient satisfaction.

Historical Charts

There are some additional techniques for displaying data on control charts that can help board members to understand the *current capability* of a process. One technique is sometimes referred to as *historical charting*. Historical charting simply means that separate means and control limits are plotted on the same chart for different time periods. They are particularly helpful when there has been a shift in a process.

Let us take a new look at two of the clinical charts we just reviewed:

- "The delay between positive mammograms and definitive biopsies" (Figure 8.11) where the process showed a positive special cause

- "Medication errors" (Figure 8.12), where there was a negative special cause

Figure 8.16 below displays the same data on "delays between mammogram and biopsy" as in Figure 8.11, but now using historical charting. The full effect of the intervention can now be assessed. The average delay improved from 30 days in 1998 to 21 days in 1999. The new process displays common cause variation and is therefore stable and predictable. In addition, the entire 1999 process was below the 1999 goal of 24 days. As more data are collected in 2000, it will be added to the 1999 data while the data from 1998 will be discarded.

Next, look at Figure 8.17. It plots the same data for "medication errors" as in Figure 8.12, now using historical charting. The full effect of assuring nurses of no reprisals can be seen more clearly. The upward shift in the process during 1999 has not leveled out as yet. The 1999 mean of 6.35/1000 orders does not tell the whole

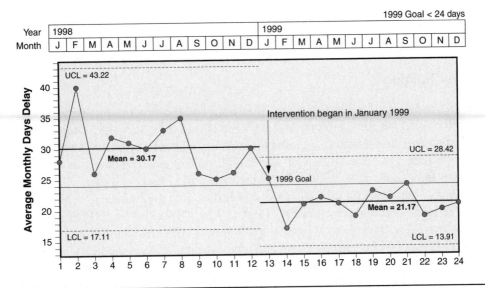

Figure 8.16 Historical chart showing the delay between positive mammogram and biopsy.
1999 process is stable and predictable with an average delay of 21 days.

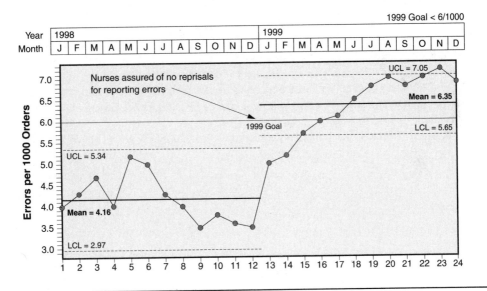

Figure 8.17 Historical chart of medication errors (errors per 1000 orders).
Error rate increased to 6.35/1000 orders, but 1999 process is still unstable and unpredictable.

story. The process is still unstable and unpredictable. As more data are collected in 2000, they would be added to the 1999 data, while the 1998 data would be dropped.

Multi-Charting

Another technique for helping board members see the relationship between various indicators is to put four or more related indicators on the same page. Doing this effectively requires that notations of interventions be omitted because the charts become much smaller. The focus here is on the overall picture and searching for relationships between indicators. This technique is sometimes called *multi-charting*. The next chart juxtaposes four financial indicators we saw earlier. It is now easier to see the relationships between "net operating margin" (Figure 8.1), "gross revenue" (Figure 8.2), "realization rate" (Figure 8.3), and "inpatient admissions" (Figure 8.4), although some of the details are lost. Net operating margin and gross revenue have increased, while the "realization rate" has remained steady and inpatient admissions have decreased.

Figure 8.19 displays the mortality rate for three processes on the same page along with a safety indicator, medication errors. These are Figures 8.6, 8.7, 8.8, and 8.17 that we have previously seen. Mortality rates have remained stable and predictable. AMI and neonatal goals for 1999 have been met, while the goal for CABG has not been met. The increase in medication errors may be due to improved reporting by the nurses.

ENDNOTES

1. R. S. Kaplan and D. P. Norton, "Using the Balanced Scorecard As a Strategic Management System," *Harvard Business Review* (January–February, 1996): 75–85.
2. C. W. Chow, et al., "The Balanced Scorecard: A Potent Tool for Energizing and Focusing Healthcare Organization Management," *Journal of Healthcare Management* 43, no. 3 (May/June 1998): 263–80.
3. R. Lawton, "Balance Your Balanced Scorecard," *ASQ Quality Progress* (March 2002): 66–71.

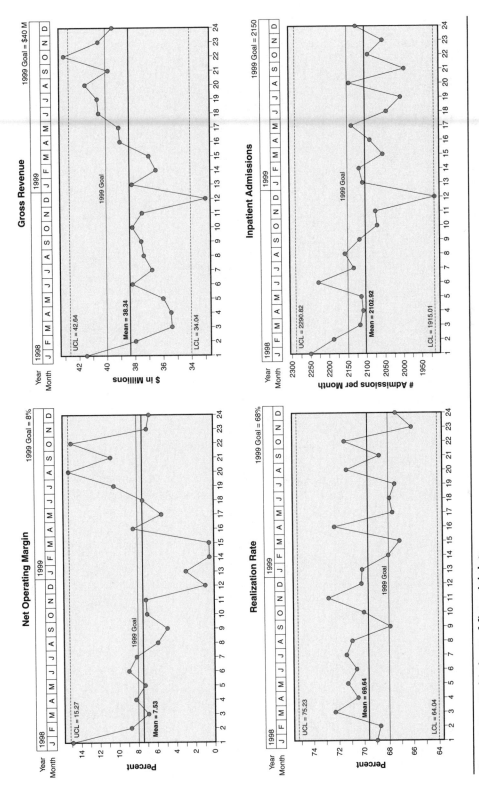

Figure 8.18   Multi-chart of financial data.

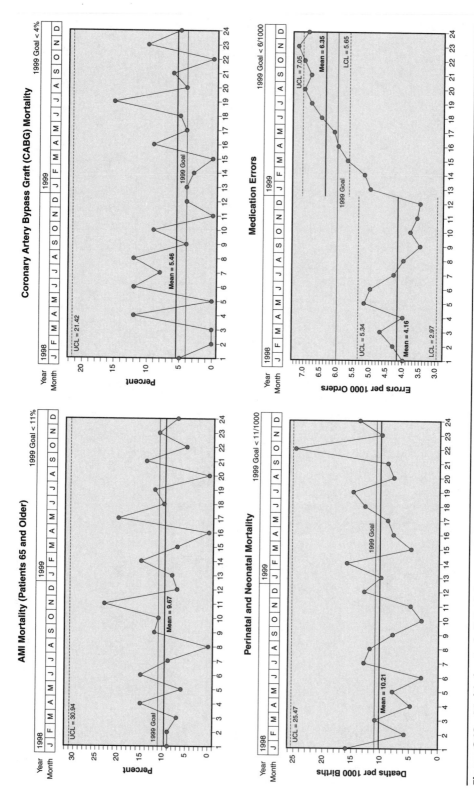

Figure 8:19 Multi-chart of clinical data.

9

Six Sigma

W hy is the subject of Six Sigma (SS) included in a book on "advanced SPC methods?" As I stated in the preface of this book, I want to address issues that cause puzzlement or confusion to those who are serious about improving healthcare processes. Because of the many articles in business and news magazines on SS, many of those attending my seminars have asked whether or not SS has a place in healthcare improvement. Specifically, I have been asked the following questions that I should like to address:

- What is Six Sigma?

- Where did it originate?

- How does it differ from SPC?

- Can it be effective in improving healthcare?

WHAT IS SIX SIGMA?

Six Sigma is both a statistic and a program.

Six Sigma as a Statistic

As a statistic, "sigma" is another word for "standard deviation," a statistical measure of the *dispersion* of a *distribution* of scores. As used in the SS program, a sigma measures the capability of a process to achieve a defect-free performance (where *defects* are defined as anything resulting in customer dissatisfaction). The ability to produce products and services with only three defects per million is described as "six sigma"—which is considered world-class performance for many processes.[1] The sigma metric is intended to serve as a common metric to compare quality across processes and across organizations.

The formula works this way. You count the number of defects in a unit (product or process) and divide it by the number of *potential* defects in the unit. That number in turn is multiplied by one million. The final result is the number of defects per million. A conversion table translates that number into sigma[2]:

- 6 sigma = 3 defects per million

- 5 sigma = 233 defects per million

- 4 sigma = 6210 defects per million

- 3 sigma = 66,807 defects per million

- 2 sigma = 308,537 defects per million

- 1 sigma = 691,462 defects per million

For example, in a hospital, if 20 food trays out of 400 were delivered "late" (by some specification limit), it would be considered as having a little better than three-sigma quality ($20/400 = .05 \times 1,000,000 = 50,000$).

In other words, as used in the SS program, sigma is a statistic that measures how well a product or service meets the customer's specifications. Specification limits express the customer's needs and, literally and figuratively, set the "goal posts" for determining defects. If a process does not function within a specified range, then a defect is said to occur. In manufacturing, specification limits are determined by engineers, and employees creating the product ensure that it falls within those parameters.

Therefore, the word "sigma" as used in the SS program does not have the same meaning as the "sigma" of a *control chart*, which is used to measure the variation of a *process* as it functions over time. With a control chart, if a point falls outside the "three-sigma line," this point is considered a "special cause" and signifies that the process is unstable and unpredictable. The formulas for the computation of the "three-sigma limits" of control charts vary with the type of control chart. (References for the formulas are listed in the appendix.)

Six Sigma As a Program

SS is also a program with its own goal, methodology, leadership training, and tools. Its primary *goal* is to improve profitability by reducing costs. In SS theory, costs are reduced by reducing defects.[3] Defects are reduced by reducing variability in a process. Defects are responsible for the "cost of poor quality."

SS has its own *methodology*, the "Breakthrough Strategy," which has eight fundamental steps or stages: recognize, define, measure, analyze, improve, control, standardize, and integrate. The methodology includes the well-known techniques of *benchmarking* and *failure mode and effects analysis* (FMEA). The Breakthrough Strategy is intended to be a "roadmap to decrease variability."

SS has developed its own *leadership training* programs. It trains individuals as Champions, Master Blackbelts, Blackbelts, and Greenbelts. Each group has its own specific role to play in implementing the Breakthrough Strategy. Harry and Schroeder (2000) explain these roles in detail in their book.[4]

Finally, SS trains its leaders to use a set of *tools*, which are not original, but rather taken from other sources: for example, process mapping, gauge R and R, and response surface (from manufacturing); analysis of variance, hypothesis testing, regression, and design of experiments (from basic research methodology); Pareto and control charts (from SPC).

ORIGIN OF THE SIX SIGMA PROGRAM

SS originated at Motorola in the early 1980s and helped the company win the 1988 Malcolm Baldrige National Quality Award. Bill Smith, a reliability engineer at Motorola, is widely credited with initiating SS and selling it to Bob Galvin, president and later chairman of Motorola. Mikel Harry was a senior staff engineer at Motorola's Government Electronics Group. In 1990 Harry started up Motorola's Six Sigma Research Institute in Schaumburg, Illinois. In 1994 Harry and Richard Schroeder, former vice president for Motorola's Codex subsidiary, began the Six Sigma Academy in Scottsdale, Arizona.

Harry and Schroeder sold the SS concept to Jack Welch of General Electric. SS received national visibility when Jack Welch made it the operating strategy at General Electric in 1995. He set the goal of having GE become a "Six Sigma quality company" by the year 2000. The goal was not reached, but GE prospered. It is hard to argue with success, but it has yet to be demonstrated whether GE's success was due to Welch's dynamic and charismatic (some would say "heavy-handed") leadership or the SS program. He served on no outside boards and devoted virtually all of his time to running GE. Welch required SS training of all employees who were on a management track. He also ranked all employees on their success in SS and tied promotion and compensation to performance. GE had spent over $300,000,000 in its quality improvement effort by 1997.[5] All of these factors may have contributed to the success of the SS program at GE.

Following GE's financial success, which many attributed to SS, other management consultants developed their own version of SS philosophy and training for manufacturing and industry. Among the most well known of these consultants is Thomas Pyzdek (Tucson, Arizona), author of *The Complete Guide to Six Sigma* (1999), and a regular contributor on SS to *Quality Digest*. His book is indeed the most complete description of SS that I have seen.

HOW DOES SIX SIGMA DIFFER FROM SPC?

SS and SPC have several things in common:

- Both focus on improving processes

- Both stress reducing process variability as a means of improving a process

- Both have a strategy to reduce variability

- Both demand strong support from the top leadership

- Both use some of the same tools, for example, Pareto charts and control charts.

They also have distinguishing features:

- *SS requires specification limits*, either set by the manufacturing engineers or the customer. The quality of a process is evaluated by its ability to meet those specification limits. However, specification limits tell us what we want the process to *do,* not how it is *actually performing.* SPC uses *control limits* to tell us how a process is *actually performing, not how we would like it to perform.* Specification limits in the form of targets and goals can be added to control charts to help set common expectations, but do not have to be present. The sigma capability does not allow prediction of how the process *will* perform.

- *In SS the assumption of process stability is critical.*[6] Without stability, one cannot reliably estimate probabilities or assign a sigma level. SPC never assumes process stability. SPC uses control charts to evaluate whether or not a process is stable, that is, whether it has common cause variation (and therefore is stable and predictable) or whether it has one or more special causes (and therefore is unstable and unpredictable). Depending on the evaluation, managers will have a different approach to improving the process. In either approach the goal is to reduce variation and move the process in the right direction.

- *Control charts can predict the future behavior of a process. Sigma levels do not.* Even when a process is stable, a sigma level is a snapshot of how "defect-free" a process is at a given moment. One cannot reliably predict how a process will behave from the sigma level. However, when a control chart has 20 or more points that show only common cause variation, one can predict the process capability under the same conditions.

- *SPC doesn't just focus on eliminating "defects" as measured by "count" data.* It doesn't convert all "measurement" data into "count" data so that defects per unit ("DPU") can be measured. It is not limited to using attribute charts (P-, C-, and U-charts) to appraise DPU and the "sigma capability" of the process. SPC can use a wide variety of control charts, including the more powerful charts for measurement data (X-bar and S- and I-charts).

- *SS requires extensive (and expensive) training programs for project leaders.* SPC requires a minimum of training and virtually no knowledge of statistics. Its tools are few and relatively simple, for example, Pareto charts, scattergrams, "fishbone diagrams," run charts, and control charts. SPC is intended to be used by employees at all levels of the organization and with varying degrees of education.

- *SS has an eight-step improvement strategy.* (See page 152.) SPC can be implemented with a simple three-step improvement strategy, as outlined in chapter 1, pages 3 and 4.

EFFECTIVENESS IN HEALTHCARE

There is no doubt that the SS program has been successful as a business for consultants. Millions of dollars have been spent implementing SS programs, mostly by large manufacturing corporations like GE and Allied Signal. The corporations that have invested heavily in SS seem for the most part to be happy with it. It apparently has been useful in industry, not only in the manufacturing of products, but also in the "soft areas," which Harry and Schroeder call "transactional services," for example, billing, claims, packaging, and so on.

But the question for the readers of this book is: "Can the SS program work in healthcare?" Phrased differently, "Is the SS program a viable alternative to the PDSA approach used in SPC?"

Let me first make some distinctions. "Healthcare" encompasses a broad range of organizations and entities devoted to healthcare delivery: not-for-profit hospitals, for-profit hospitals, VA hospitals, long-term care facilities, nursing homes, physician groups of various types and sizes—to name a few in the United States. In Canada and Europe, healthcare takes the form of socialized medicine in one form or other. My own personal experience with quality improvement efforts has been mainly with not-for-profit hospitals and physician groups. My comments, therefore, reflect the limits of my experience.

It is my opinion that in some circumstances the SS *statistic* can be used to assess transactional (operational) processes in hospitals or physician offices, as well as to assess the process capability of individual patients (as Dr. Staker demonstrates in chapter 10). However, the SS statistic will not be useful to compare quality (that is, process capability) between providers or between organizations. Second, Six Sigma as a *program* is not likely to be widely used except in large healthcare systems. There are a number of reasons for these conclusions.

Setting Specification Limits

One of the main problems with using the SS *statistic* in healthcare is that it is difficult to set true "specification limits" for most clinical processes. For example, one cannot set specification limits for C-sections, or for mortalities following operative procedures. There are too many variables that need to be considered. Risk adjustment is a necessity for mortality and most outcome measures. Even where specification limits are set (somewhat arbitrarily) for some operational processes (for example, time from admission to the ED to the administration of thrombolytic therapy), it is better to assess process improvement using measurement data (that is, actual time in minutes) than using count data (that is, the target time was met or not met). This issue was addressed in chapter 6.

However, we can set arbitrary "specification limits" for a number of other operational processes, such as cycle times for lab tests and billing. We can also view goals for patient satisfaction scores as "specification limits." Estimating process capability using the sigma statistic in these instances can be appropriate as long as everyone involved agrees on the "specification limits."

In chapter 10, Dr. Larry Staker also shows how the sigma statistic can be used in clinical practice to assess the baseline performance and amount of improvement with *individual patients*. He sets his specification limits for various types of patients based on his clinical judgment. For example, for diabetic patients, fasting blood sugar should be < 110; for diabetic patients with hypertension, the systolic blood pressure (BP) should be < 130 and a diastolic (BP) should be < 85; for patients with coronary disease, LDL should be < 100; for patients with prosthetic valves being treated with Warfarin, the INR should be between 2.5 and 3.5. If used in conjunction with control charts to confirm process stability, the sigma statistic can be an acceptable tool for individual physicians to measure their degree of success in meeting their own goals with their own patients.

However, one must exercise caution if the sigma statistic is used to *compare* clinical processes between different physicians or patients. First, the processes being compared must use the *same* specification limits. Second, the sigma statistic assumes that the processes being compared are *stable*, that is, have only common cause variation. And finally, the sigma statistic makes a judgment about the current state of a process, but cannot be used to *predict* future performance.

Hospital Organization versus Industry

Not-for-profit hospitals have a different organizational structure than industrial corporations. Not everyone who works in a hospital is an employee of the hospital. Hospitals hire nurses and other clinical and nonclinical support staff. The physicians have primary responsibility for the patients, but are not employees and do not report to the administration. Physicians care for their patients in their own offices and, when necessary, bring their patients to a hospital, where both are "customers" or "guests" of the hospital staff. As a result of this organizational structure, CEOs in not-for-profit hospitals do not have the power of CEOs in industry. Hospital CEOs cannot mandate that everyone become a "quality lunatic" as Jack Welch did at GE.

Improving Profitability

As was stated earlier in this chapter, the primary goal of the SS program is to improve profitability by reducing costs. In SS theory, costs are reduced by reducing defects. However, quality improvement in a hospital setting will not be primarily motivated by cost cutting. Because both hospitals and physician groups often see money spent on improving quality as coming out of the bottom line, rather than contributing to it, there is less willingness to commit time and money to improving care.

Quality improvement initiatives in hospitals will generally be initiated either by the:

- Professional dedication of administration and physicians to provide the best quality patients

- Fear of losing patients to competitors

- Need to meet accreditation requirements

- Fear of lawsuits

Since 1990, both managed care and Medicare reimbursement have done a great deal to "squeeze the fat" out of healthcare. General public opinion may not agree, but the move to consolidate is a testimony to the financial pressures on hospitals and physicians. The stand-alone community hospital and the solo physician practitioner are becoming as rare as bison on the American scene.

SPC versus Six Sigma

In conclusion, the SS program, as it is currently propagated by consultants such as Harry and Schroeder at the Six Sigma Academy and by Pyzdek, theoretically has the potential of being as effective for transactional processes in hospitals and in physician offices as it has been in industrial settings. However, the unique organizational structure and financial reimbursement mechanisms in healthcare will not allow SS to become a viable quality improvement strategy in most situations. A few large healthcare systems may be the exception.

There are also workable and less costly alternatives. The "Breakthrough Series" organized by the Institute for Healthcare Improvement (Boston, Massachusetts) provides a national forum to assist both hospital leadership and physicians in improving healthcare processes, for example, reducing medication errors, improving accessibility and functioning of physician offices, and improving emergency department care. Smaller hospitals can implement SPC with a modest outlay of time and resources. The PDSA cycle of Shewhart/Deming is a workable strategy for every type of healthcare process. The SPC tools are adequate to implement this strategy and require much less time and resources than are required to implement an SS program.

ENDNOTES

1. R. D. Snee, "Why Should Statisticians Pay Attention to Six Sigma?" *ASQ Quality Progress* (September 1999): 100.
2. These figures are taken from the Six Sigma Conversion Table at the end of the book *Six Sigma* (2000) by Mikel Harry and Richard Schroeder. This table includes a 1.5 sigma shift for all listed values of Z.
3. M. Harry and R. Schroeder, *Six Sigma* (New York: Currency, 2000): 20–21.
4. Ibid., 172–75.
5. J. Erwin, "Achieving Total Customer Satisfaction through Six Sigma," *Quality Digest* (July 1998): 39.
6. J. S. Ramburg, "Six Sigma: Fad or Fundamental?" *Quality Digest* (May 2000): 29.

10

The Use of Run and Control Charts in the Improvement of Clinical Practice

by Larry V. Staker, MD, FACP

Physicians trained to care for patients as individuals are often intimidated by the task of measurement. They recognize that many guidelines for patient care learned during residency and practiced for years eventually support outdated systems of care. Clinicians may not recognize the power of using simple measurement tools or their ability to influence, change, and improve clinical practice with tools like run charts and control charts that have been previously documented in this book.

EVALUATING BASELINE PERFORMANCE

To begin any type of clinical improvement, evaluation of baseline performance is necessary. Baseline data are usually available in the clinical record, but may not be easily accessible or in the best format. So the first challenge is collecting, formatting, validating, and analyzing baseline data.

Diabetes mellitus is a common serious chronic condition with costly co-morbidities,[1] which will serve as an example for learning the basic skills of measurement and analysis and applying them in a clinical setting. The first step in evaluating baseline performance is to determine a clear goal by deciding what to measure (that is, the key outcome variable or KOV) and setting a standard for performance (that is, specification limits or SLs). For example, in diabetes care the goal is to improve the care of all patients in a practice with Type 2 diabetes by getting their fasting blood sugar (FBS) to ≤ 110 and their hemoglobin A1c (HbA1c) to ≤ 7.0. In this written statement the population to be studied is defined, the KOVs selected for measurement are identified as FBS and HbA1c, and the standard of care (or specification limit) is clearly stated.

The second step in baseline evaluation is the collection of baseline data. This step is often done by chart review. The information needed is patient identification, date of service, and result of FBS and/or HbA1c. The data may be recorded by hand in a data collection table or entered into a spreadsheet. Table 10.1 is an example of a data collection table.

A primary care internist would typically care for 100 to 150 patients with Type 2 diabetes. A difficulty often first encountered is the identification of all the patients in the practice with diabetes. Sometimes the best way to start to find these patients is to just begin data collection, identifying the diabetics each day as they come in for routine visits. In this manner a valid sample for baseline data can be acquired in three to six months. Some doctors are fortunate enough to have electronic medical records, which make identification of patients with a specific diagnosis easier. Other means of identifying the patient population include searching billing information for the ICD9 code (#250 for diabetes), finding patients who have had an HbA1c ordered, or asking the pharmacy for a list of patients who have filled prescriptions for insulin or oral hypoglycemic agents. If patients are identified in this manner, a rapid and focused chart review can be initiated to collect the baseline data. For an average primary care internist's practice, the baseline data will generally consist of 200–300 observations per year.

The third step in evaluating baseline data is assessing baseline "process capability"[2] and setting goals for treatment. One of the most helpful ways of looking at baseline data is to create a histogram. If the data has been entered in a spreadsheet such as Excel, then the histogram can be created using the charting function.

Figure 10.1 shows glycemic control in diabetes monitored with fasting blood sugar (FBS) and with hemoglobin A1c (HbA1c or A1c). Side-by-side comparison of histograms of these two tests (FBS and A1c) done in a population of 100 patients with diabetes over a two-year period (1992–1994) shows mean values of 187 and 10.5 respectively. Acceptable control before publication of the DCCT and UKPDS randomized control trials should have been reflected in mean values of 140 and 8.5 respectively. These histograms send a clear message of the need for improvement in ambulatory diabetes care.[3]

A histogram can also be easily created by hand. To do an analysis by hand of fasting glucose in a population, first create a number of "bins" covering the range of FBS values collected. Then count the number of observations that fall in each "bin," marking each data point with an "x." The resulting frequency plot is really a handmade histogram (Table 10.2).

Table 10.1 Sample data collection table.

Patient ID	Date of Service	HbA1c	FBS
100001	05/01/01	7.0	110
159633	02/02/01	8.2	145
122368	06/07/00	6.8	108
100001	03/09/00	8.9	150
226432	09/08/99	7.5	135
147222	08/13/99	7.4	134
134922	03/15/00	7.0	112
561377	02/01/99	8.4	146
226432	01/15/99	11.0	250

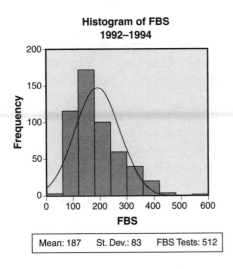

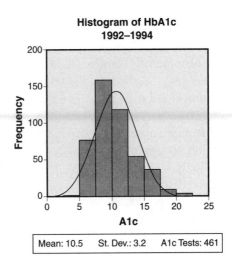

Figure 10.1　Histograms of FBS and HbA1c for 100 patients.

Table 10.2　Handmade histogram of FBS for 142 diabetic patients.

Bin	Frequency or Count	Total	
50–59	x	1	Histogram created by hand in a population of patients with Type 2 diabetes mellitus.
60–69	x x	2	
70–79	x	1	
80–89	x x x	3	
90–99	x x x x	4	
100–109	x x x x x	5	
110–119	x x x x x x	6	
120–129	x x x x x x x	7	
139–139	x x x x x x x x x	9	
140–149	x x x x x x x x x x x	11	
150–159	x x x x x x x x x x x x	12	
160–169	x x x x x x x x x x x x x	13	
170–179	x x x x x x x x x x x x x	13	
180–189	x x x x x x x x x x x x	12	
190–199	x x x x x x x x x x	10	
200–209	x x x x x x x x	8	
210–219	x x x x x x x	7	
220–229	x x x x x x	6	
230–239	x x x x	4	
240–249	x x x	3	
250–259	x x	2	
260–269	x	1	
270–279		0	
280–289	x	1	
290–299	x	1	

If the same data had been entered in a spreadsheet such as Excel, making a column or bar chart of the "total" column using the charting or graphing function will also create the histogram.[4] Other useful information from the chart in Table 10.2 includes the sum of the "total" column or the total number counted (142), the number < 110 (16), and the number ≥ 110 (126).

Figure 10.2 is a computer-generated histogram of data in Table 10.2 showing baseline data from a population of 142 with FBS levels grouped and counted in "bins." In this case the histogram approximates a normal distribution. A mean value can be estimated visually and that mean can be mentally compared with the standard of care for this practice (FBS < 110).

In this example of 142 patients, both the handmade and the Excel-generated histograms appear to be very close to a normal distribution. However, the mean fasting blood sugar (FBS) is about 170. If the standard of care for this practice is an FBS of less than 110, there is definitely room for improvement. The process of care should therefore be carefully analyzed and changes should be made in this process that will move the mean FBS from 170 toward 110. Repeating and comparing histograms over time could demonstrate the success of these changes, but run charts and control charts are really better for this kind of analysis over time.

Baseline data gives a starting place and a reference point for comparison. It is the first principle of improvement and is absolutely necessary, for without it one cannot really tell whether a change in the process of care results in an improvement.

For example, the three totals from the handmade frequency chart are: 1) 142, or the total number of patients (denominator); 2) 16, or the total number treated to goal (TTG), namely those with an FBS < 110; and 3) 126, or the total number not treated to goal (NTTG). By entering these numbers into an Excel-based analysis tool (Figure 10.3) one can easily understand the baseline performance level and what will be needed to get a

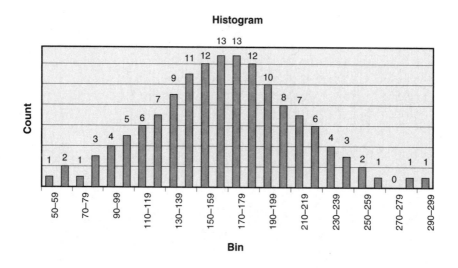

Figure 10.2 Computer-generated histogram of FBS for 142 diabetic patients.

twofold and a tenfold improvement in clinical outcome as reflected in the key outcome variable (FBS). In other words, at baseline 126 of 142 patients are not treated to goal, namely those with a FBS > 110. If the goal of the improvement effort were a twofold improvement in number not treated to goal, then 63 of 142 patients should be NTTG. A tenfold improvement would mean that only 13 of the 142 patients would be NTTG.

Figure 10.3 describes two methods for assessing baseline "process capability" and setting goals: the percent treated to goal (TTG) and Six Sigma statistic (described earlier in chapter 9).

In Figure 10.3, N = numerator, or in this case number not treated to goal (# NTTG). D = denominator, or total number counted. DPMO = defects per million observations. M = one million. TTG = percent of observed population treated to goal. NTTG = percent of observed population not treated to goal. SIGMA = a number from zero to six that describes the DPMO. The closer the number approaches to six, the better the outcome or performance. The "Sigma" performance level of any process can be calculated using the Excel function NORMSINV(1-(N/D))+1.5 where "N" and "D" are defined as noted above. In improving clinical practice, either the TTG or Sigma methods can be useful in setting goals for process change.

Caution should be exercised when using either the TTG percent or sigma statistic to compare two different processes. Both methods require that the *same specification limit* be used for both processes being compared. In addition, the sigma statistic also *assumes that both processes are stable*, that is, have only common cause variation. (The assumption of process stability with the sigma statistic was discussed in chapter 9.) *Neither* the TTG nor sigma statistic can be used to *predict the future behavior* of a process.

In summary, the three steps of baseline evaluation are: 1) determination of a clear goal by deciding what to measure (the KOVs) and setting a standard for performance, 2) collection of the baseline data, and 3) assessing the baseline process capability and setting treatment goals.

enter numerator (# NTTG) and denominator (total # of Patients) in marked fields						
Numerator:	126			**Denominator:**	142	
N	**D**	**DPMO**	**M**	**TTG**	**NTTG**	**SIGMA**
BASELINE PERFORMANCE						
126	142	887324	1000000	11.27%	88.73%	0.3
TENFOLD IMPROVEMENT						
13	142	88732	1000000	91.13%	8.87%	2.8
TWOFOLD IMPROVEMENT						
63	142	443662	1000000	55.63%	44.37%	1.6

Figure 10.3 Excel-based tool for assessing baseline performance and setting improvement goals.

DISPLAYING THE DATA GRAPHICALLY

Returning now to the baseline population measurement of 100 diabetic patients displayed in Figure 10.1, the mean FBS was 187 and the mean HbA1c was 10.5. Building on the concepts outlined above, the 100 patients with diabetes were taught to do daily self-monitoring of blood glucose (SMBG) using a glucometer and were given a simple graphic measurement tool called a "diabetes specification chart." This chart is a line graph of data collected over time, with superimposed horizontal lines indicating a range of allowable variation labeled upper (USL) and lower specification limits (LSL). It may also contain a horizontal line near the center (CL) of that range that represents the goal of treatment. An example of the diabetes specification chart is shown in Figure 10.4.

Patients were instructed to plot daily glucometer readings for fasting blood sugar on these specification charts and to bring them to their follow-up visits. The numbers on the X-axis correspond to days of the month, and those on the Y-axis correspond to blood sugar. Using clinical judgment, the upper specification limit (USL) was set at 130 and the lower specification limit (LSL) at 90. The center specification (CS), or centerline (CL), is the treatment goal of fasting blood sugar of 110. The grid lines assist patients in plotting. In this manner the patients are taught the fundamentals of acceptable variation and are given a clear understanding of the goal for glycemic control. Similar reasoning could be used to develop specification charts for such clinical indicators as peak flow rates in asthma, systolic and diastolic blood pressure in hypertension, and so on.

In small group sessions, patients were taught the basic elements of good diabetes care and the proper technique for measuring and recording daily blood glucose levels on the diabetes specification chart. The burden of data collection was thus delegated by empowering the patients to measure and plot their results graphically. The patients were

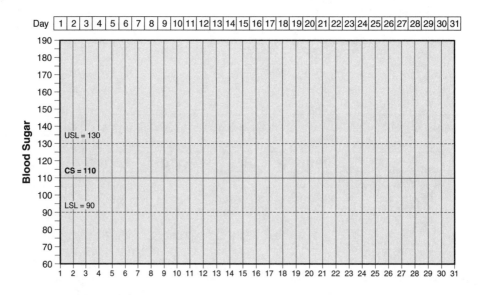

Figure 10.4   Diabetes specification chart.

then asked to bring their completed specification charts with them to their follow-up visits. An example of a patient-generated diabetes specification chart containing data is shown in Figure 10.5.

Patient self-monitored blood glucose (SMBG) data recorded on a diabetes specification chart (data plotted in time sequence and grid lines removed) allow rapid and accurate evaluation of effectiveness of treatment over time. Both physicians and patients become proficient at understanding care process stability and the importance of treatment to goal. Communication between patient and physician about the key outcome variable (fasting blood sugar) is improved and rapid daily feedback supports positive behavior. This empowers patients to both understand and manage their diabetes. This patient is obviously not treated to the goal of FBS < 110, but his FBS has improved. More intensive therapy is indicated.

A clinician familiar with run charts and run chart rules would convert the specification chart (Figure 10.5) into a run chart (Figure 10.6). The first six data points were excluded in calculating the median because they were part of an old process of care. The remaining 25 points were graphed on the run chart displayed as Figure 10.6.

Patient self-monitored blood glucose (SMBG) data converted from a diabetes specification chart to a run chart allows rapid, accurate, and more sophisticated evaluation of the process of treatment over time. The run chart in Figure 10.6 shows that after the new process of care was initiated on day seven, the process was stable, but unacceptable. The process is stable because the run chart tests for a special cause (see chapter 1) did not identify any special causes. The process is unacceptable because 22 of the 25 FBS readings were above the specification limit (110). (See Figure 10.5.) A clinician seeing this pattern would review the use of the measurement tool, educate the patient on diet and exercise, check the glucometer, and adjust the medication. The specification chart

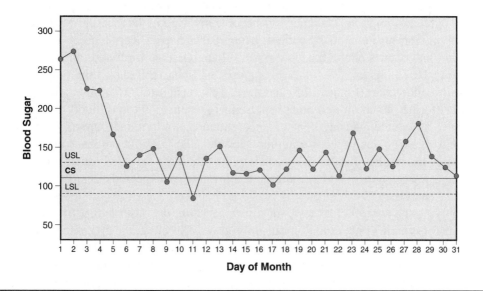

Figure 10.5 Patient-generated diabetes specification chart.

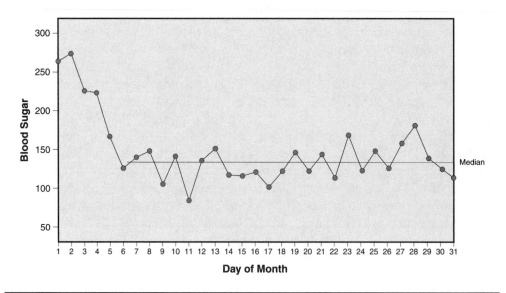

Figure 10.6   Diabetes run chart.

next month would be converted into a run chart and would be evaluated and compared with this one. These "rapid cycles" could be repeated monthly until the run chart showed a stable and acceptable process of care.

Prior to self-measurement and plotting data graphically, the diabetic patient might have spent 15 minutes four times a year with a physician receiving feedback about the disease. Using a diabetes specification chart, the patient *may now spend 5 minutes each day measuring, plotting, and receiving feedback* about blood sugar control. Fifteen hours of feedback per year versus one hour of feedback per year. Is it any wonder that clinical outcomes improve when patients become involved in the measurement process?

Individual measurements by patients using diabetic specification charts can also be converted into control charts for more powerful analysis, as illustrated in Figure 10.7.

Figure 10.7 is an *Individuals control chart* (or I-chart). It shows the same data as the specification chart (Figure 10.5) and the run chart (Figure 10.6) converted into control chart format. Each plotted point represents one self-monitored blood sugar value, that is, 31 individual measurements. Hence, the term "Individuals" chart. An individuals control chart displays a key outcome variable (FBS) in time sequence order (day). The centerline on the chart is the mean value of the data set. UCL and LCL are the upper and lower control limits, indicating the range of expected variation based on statistical analysis.[5]

Applying the control chart tests for a special cause, we observe that from day 7 to 31 this process shows only common cause variation. Therefore, the process is stable and predictable. However, it is still unacceptable because only three of 25 days during the new process period were below the specification limit (110). The control chart reached the same conclusion as the run chart regarding the stability of the process. However, the UCL and LCL also give us the ability to predict the expected variation in the process.

Day	1	2	3	4	5	6	7	8	9	10	11	12	13	14	15	16	17	18	19	20	21	22	23	24	25	26	27	28	29	30	31
1	260	278	230	225	165	130	146	158	108	145	80	144	160	122	122	126	98	126	150	126	148	114	168	122	154	126	160	188	144	126	118

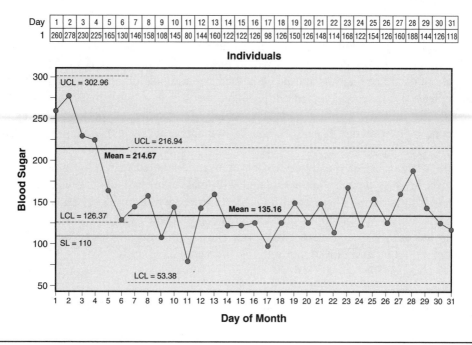

Figure 10.7   I-chart for FBS.

Graphical display of patient self-measurement of fasting plasma glucose connects both the patient and the physician with the management of diabetes. It clearly emphasizes the dual role of the patients as measurers and providers of their own self-care while empowering them with information helpful to their physicians. Patients using this measurement tool are motivated and better equipped to make judgments regarding diet, exercise, compliance, treatment changes, and overall control of their diabetes. They begin to request visits with other members of the diabetes care team, such as diabetes educators and dieticians. They understand that better control of blood sugar will prevent complications of their disease, and they begin to ask questions about the appropriate use of their medications. Return visits do not take any more time than they did before the intervention, but the review of diabetic specification charts with the physician becomes an expected and important part of the care system.

Patients become adept at reporting the reasons for values outside of specification limits and understand more about how their own behavior influences their diabetes. This simple change in measurement and feedback resulted in diabetic patients being more involved in their own care and more aware of the direct correlation between their day-to-day behavior and the control of their disease. The diabetes specification chart is an effective, inexpensive, simple measurement tool that leads to sustainable measurable outcome improvements. Clinicians can enhance their ability to interpret and learn from the data collected by the patient by converting it into a run chart or a control chart.

Of the 100 patients taught to do self-monitoring of blood glucose and to use the diabetes specification chart for graphical display, 90 percent continued to record daily

SMBG values at the end of one year, and 85 percent of them continued to use this technique of self-measurement and feedback for the next five years.

In clinical practice, if physicians would place specification charts in the hands of their patients and use them in routine care, then communication and compliance would both improve. Diseases associated with reliable measurement tools that can be used by patients after minimal training include diabetes (glucometer), hypertension (devices that record blood pressure digitally), weight management (scales), asthma (peak flow meters), and so on.

Other conditions, such as hyperlipidemia or anticoagulation, require more innovative efforts because they are not associated with measurement tools that can be placed in the hands of patients. These conditions are followed by lab results (LDL-C or INR), which are readily available to the physician but can be made available to the patient. To facilitate the use of specification charts, run charts, and control charts for cholesterol management, let us turn our attention to the following case study.

CASE STUDY #1: CHOLESTEROL MANAGEMENT

The Situation

After developing angina, a 78-year-old retired professor had a myocardial infarction (MI) in 1993 and a three-vessel coronary artery bypass graft (CABG). The problem is to monitor and determine the effectiveness of the management of his cholesterol in the prevention of future coronary events. Data have been collected over time since 1992. The baseline evaluation consists of all data from 1992 to 1996. Statins were available in 1992, but were not widely used until the publication of the "4S" clinical trial in 1995.[6] The complete data set is shown in Table 10.3.

The first question to be addressed is: "Which of the variables should be the key outcome variable (KOV)?" The 4S clinical trial reported reduction of LDL cholesterol after the use of Simvastatin, so the selection of LDL as the KOV makes sense. This should allow the comparison of clinical response to the results published in the paper. The patient's LDL data from Table 10.3 are displayed in the specification chart in Figure 10.8.

In this LDL-C specification chart (Figure 10.8), one can clearly see that all but seven of the LDL-C values are above the specification limit of LDL-C ≤ 100. Visual inspection makes one think that there are two processes of care, one accounting for data points one to five and another for the rest. There is one point near the end that seems out of place. The centerline is not necessary in a specification chart, but is convenient if the analysis is to be taken to the next level, run chart analysis.

Specification charts allow one to numerically estimate "process capability." For example, seven observations out of 24 were under the specification limit (100). Therefore, the "process capability" as estimated by the TTG ratio is 7/24, or 29 percent. Stated in another way, one could say that this data set shows the overall process of care is capable of treatment to goal only 29 percent of the time.

Table 10.3 Cholesterol profile for 78-year-old male patient.

PN	Date	TCHOL	LDL	HDL	TRIG	VLDL
10059	7/8/1992	234	174	37	114	23
10059	9/24/1992	248	176	43	147	32
10059	3/16/1993	303	221	39	217	43
10059	6/29/1993	278	191	37	252	50
10059	9/9/1994	274	209	42	117	23
10059	10/17/1994	195	106	50	194	39
10059	3/7/1995	217	141	43	166	33
10059	10/25/1995	196	116	56	122	24
10059	2/27/1996	164	104	40	98	20
10059	6/25/1996	164	106	38	106	21
10059	9/25/1996	156	94	43	97	19
10059	2/26/1997	173	103	48	112	22
10059	6/9/1997	164	103	42	96	19
10059	9/9/1997	199	128	39	159	32
10059	10/27/1997	150	87	38	123	25
10059	12/16/1997	165	97	36	160	32
10059	3/5/1998	197	120	40	185	37
10059	5/26/1998	169	104	49	78	16
10059	8/27/1998	144	86	45	66	13
10059	10/29/1998	188	123	47	91	18
10059	2/8/1999	287	215	41	154	31
10059	3/9/1999	168	97	48	117	23
10059	6/7/1999	149	88	40	103	21
10059	12/13/1999	141	80	48	65	13

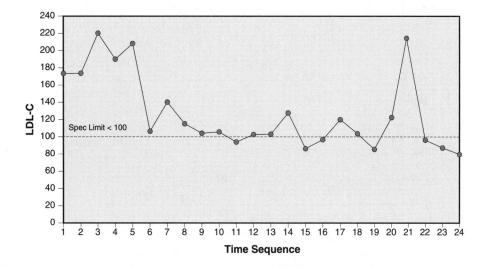

Figure 10.8 **Specification chart for LDL data of 78-year-old male patient.**

The data in Table 10.3 could also be made into a run chart (see Figure 10.9). This is best done with the assistance of some software, but can also be done by hand.

Visual inspection of the data in Figure 10.9 helps one see that there are really two processes of care in this case. Therefore, the two processes have been separated and a median has been calculated for each data set: 191 and 104 respectively. The specification

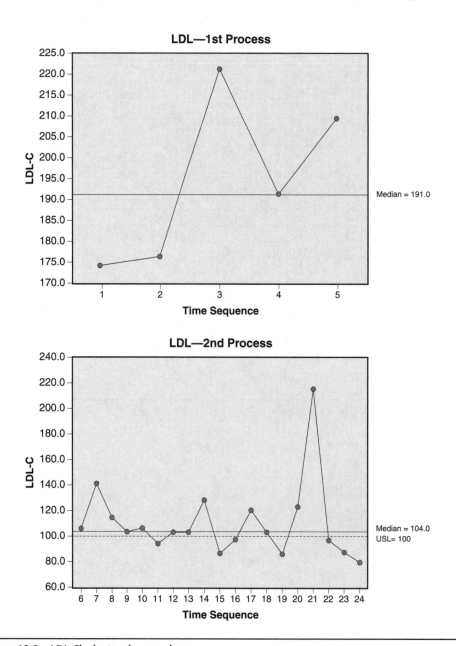

Figure 10.9   LDL Cholesterol—run charts.

limit (100) has been superimposed on the run chart for the second process. What is the percent treated to goal (TTG) in the second process? The answer is 7/19, or 36.8 percent.

Control chart analysis adds additional information of help to the clinician. Note that control charts can be used to display baseline data in place of the histograms described early in this chapter. The chart on the left in Figure 10.10 is an example of baseline data displayed in control chart format. It serves as a reference for comparison with the chart on the right. Specification limits can also be superimposed on control charts, but tend to clutter the graph.

The control chart in Figure 10.10 is an Individuals, or I-chart. The chart on the right clearly signals special cause variation because point 21 lies beyond the UCL. It was not possible to clearly identify this point as a special cause in Figure 10.9 when using the run chart tests. The appropriate course of action is to identify the reason for the special cause and try to eliminate it. The physician should not change the process of care until the cause of the special cause has been identified.

Figure 10.11 shows the moving range (MR) chart that is sometimes displayed along with the individuals chart. Notice that no new information is provided by the MR chart, and it might even cause confusion. There are two points above the UCL of the MR chart, not one point as we observed in the I-chart (Figure 10.10). This is because point 21 on the I-chart was separated from the preceding point (20) and the following point (22) by a sizeable difference. Nevertheless, only point 21 was the special cause.

Test	1	2	3	4	5	6	7	8	9	10	11	12	13	14	15	16	17	18	19	20	21	22	23	24
LDL	174.2	175.6	220.6	190.6	208.6	106.2	140.8	115.6	104.0	106.0	94.0	103.0	103.0	128.0	87.0	97.0	120.0	104.0	86.0	123.0	215.0	97.0	88.0	80.0

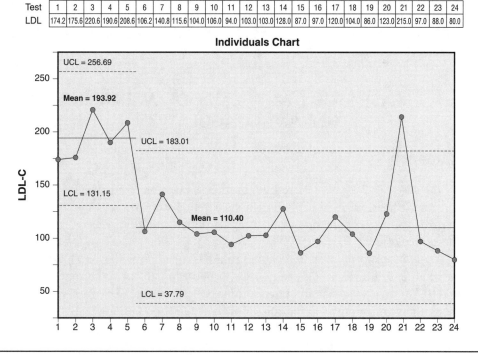

Figure 10.10   LDL cholesterol (I-chart).

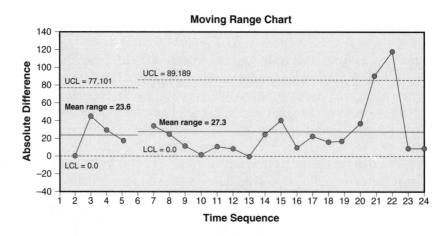

Figure 10.11   LDL cholesterol—moving range chart.

How, then, are we to assess the effectiveness of care over time given to this man with coronary artery disease (CAD)? Note that his LDL-C shows a definite change in late 1995 (point 6) on both the run chart and the I-chart. This is when Simvastatin was introduced with the support of the Scandinavian Simvastatin Survival Study (4S). The data show definite improvement in the patient's LDL-C with movement toward National Cholesterol Education Project (NCEP)–suggested goals for patients with CAD. However, the patient is still not consistently treated to goal. There is room for improvement. His current therapy is capable of reaching the treatment goal (LDL-C < 100) only 36.8 percent of the time.

CASE STUDY #2: THE USE OF WARFARIN FOR ANTICOAGULATION

The Situation

This is the case of a 72-year-old retired attorney who is anticoagulated with Warfarin for a prosthetic heart valve to prevent embolic cerebral vascular accident and stroke. As an internist, you are compulsive about keeping anticoagulation records, so they are a reliable source of data.

One could look at the baseline data (Table 10.4) with a histogram, but the sample size is small and a histogram is not likely to be very helpful. What does an I-chart (Figure 10.12) or a specification chart (Figure 10.13) show? The I-chart shows that this patient has an average international normalized ratio (INR) of 3.32. The process of anticoagulation seems to be fairly stable, except for point three which is a single point beyond the UCL, indicating a special cause variation. One should seek for an explanation of this value before changing the Warfarin dosage. Further investigation revealed that the patient had one GI bleed at time three, as well as a TIA at time 19.

Table 10.4   Anticoagulation case study: baseline data.

PN	TS	Date	PT	INR	Dose/Wk
10633	1	11/14/1994	19.6	2.9	20.3
10633	2	11/15/1994	19.6	2.9	20.3
10633	3	11/29/1994	27.9	6.0	22.5
10633	4	12/15/1994	19.5	2.8	22.5
10633	5	12/29/1994	18.8	2.7	27.5
10633	6	1/12/1995	24.2	4.7	22.5
10633	7	1/26/1995	21.8	3.7	22.5
10633	8	2/9/1995	20.9	3.4	22.5
10633	9	3/8/1995	20.7	3.3	23.1
10633	10	3/23/1995	17.5	2.3	16.1
10633	11	3/28/1995	17.7	2.6	22.5
10633	12	4/18/1995	18.8	2.9	22.5
10633	13	5/10/1995	20.1	3.4	22.5
10633	14	6/21/1995	20.1	3.4	22.5
10633	15	7/5/1995	20.9	3.7	25.9
10633	16	7/19/1995	15.8	2.0	14.0
10633	17	8/4/1995	18.1	2.7	18.9
10633	18	8/29/1995	19.8	3.3	23.1
10633	19	9/28/1995	15.0	1.8	12.6
10633	20	10/24/1995	23.5	4.7	32.9
10633	21	11/22/1995	21.2	3.8	26.6
10633	22	12/21/1995	19.9	2.7	18.9
10633	23	1/23/1996	21.4	3.2	22.4
10633	24	2/22/1996	21.1	3.1	21.7
10633	25	3/20/1996	26.0	5.0	35.0

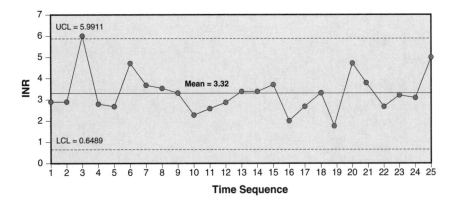

Figure 10.12   Anticoagulation—individuals chart.

Times 10 through 15 are six steadily ascending values, but are one point short of the seven required for a special cause.

The specification chart (Figure 10.13) displays the national treatment guideline of an INR between 2.5 to 3.5 for patients with prosthetic valves. The patient's average INR (3.32) falls within these specification limits. However, the control limits in Figure 10.12 are a lot wider than the specification limits. Analysis of the baseline data set demonstrates that the baseline process is capable of treatment to goal only 60 percent of the time (that is, 15 of 25 INR readings being within the SLs of 2.5 to 3.5). The process needs to be studied and improved.

Baseline analysis of the anticoagulation records in a group of nine internists led to two major conclusions: 1) tampering or changing the Warfarin dose too frequently accounts for increased variation in INR and decreased capability to treat patients to goal, and 2) because the specification limits of the process lay inside the three-sigma control limits, it is unlikely that the patients can be treated to goal 100 percent of the time. The best TTG outcome that can be expected is 70 percent to 75 percent.

If the specification limits lay within the control limits, then it is necessary to challenge the appropriateness of the specification limits. After continued careful study of the anticoagulation process, the internists determined that as long as the INR was not less than or greater than 0.5 on either side of the nationally accepted specification limit, the dose of Warfarin would not be changed. Close inspection of the baseline data in Table 10.4 shows a good deal of variation in Warfarin doses. Notice the decrease in the variation of Warfarin doses in the follow-up data set in Table 10.5.

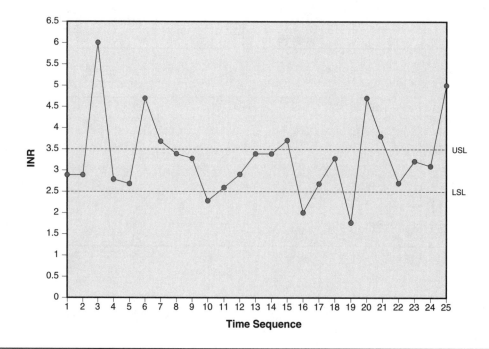

Figure 10.13   Specification chart of the anticoagulation baseline data.

Another piece of useful information that can be obtained from the baseline data is the Six Sigma calculation, which is the second method of assessing process capability used by the internists. It is illustrated in Figure 10.14.

Figure 10.14 shows that the baseline performance has a 40 percent error rate with respect to treatment to goal (TTG). This would be rated as a 1.8 sigma process. A twofold improvement would bring it to 2.3 sigma, or a 20 percent error rate. A tenfold improvement would bring it to 3.3 sigma, or a 4 percent error rate.

The data after the process change are shown in Table 10.5. The best way to see what occurred after the change in treatment guidelines is to look at the two control charts (before and after the change) side by side (Figure 10.15).

Figure 10.15 is an historical I-chart showing baseline data on the left and data after process change on the right. The classic signs of improvement are a movement in the

Table 10.5 Anticoagulation data set after change in treatment guidelines.

PN	TS	Date	PT	INR	Dose/Wk
10633	26	4/2/1996	19.1	2.5	17.5
10633	27	4/29/1996	22.3	3.5	22.5
10633	28	5/21/1996	21.9	3.4	22.5
10633	29	6/4/1996	19.6	2.7	22.5
10633	30	7/1/1996	22.3	3.5	22.5
10633	31	8/2/1996	20.3	2.9	22.5
10633	32	8/29/1996	19.6	2.7	22.5
10633	33	10/1/1996	21.6	3.3	22.5
10633	34	11/7/1996	22.8	3.1	22.5
10633	35	12/11/1996	19.4	2.3	22.5
10633	36	1/21/1997	21.6	3.6	22.5
10633	37	1/28/1997	18.3	2.6	22.5
10633	38	3/7/1997	17.1	2.3	22.5
10633	39	4/9/1997	19.4	2.9	22.5
10633	40	5/9/1997	18.1	2.5	22.5
10633	41	7/2/1997	19.4	2.8	0.0
10633	42	7/23/1997	18.8	2.9	22.5
10633	43	9/12/1997	18.8	2.8	22.5
10633	44	11/13/1997	19.1	3.0	22.5
10633	45	1/8/1998	16.6	2.1	22.5
10633	46	4/28/1998	19.2	2.9	22.5
10633	47	6/5/1998	20.1	3.2	22.5
10633	48	7/15/1998	18.0	2.5	22.5
10633	49	9/24/1998	18.3	2.6	22.5
10633	50	12/15/1998	16.8	2.0	22.5
10633	51	12/15/1998	17.4	2.3	22.5
10633	52	7/28/1999	17.2	2.3	22.5
10633	53	10/11/1999	20.8	3.0	22.5
10633	54	5/25/2000	17.7	2.2	22.5

N	D	DPMO	M	TTG	NTTG	SIGMA
enter numerator (# NTTG) and denominator (# total) in the appropriate fields						
Numerator: 10				**Denominator:** 25		
BASELINE PERFORMANCE						
10	25	400000	1000000	60.00%	40.00%	1.8
TENFOLD IMPROVEMENT						
1	25	40000	1000000	96.00%	4.00%	3.3
TWOFOLD IMPROVEMENT						
5	25	200000	1000000	80.00%	20.00%	2.3

Figure 10.14 Evaluation of baseline process performance using TTG and Six Sigma.

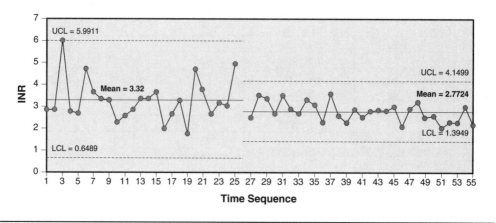

Figure 10.15 Anticoagulation Individuals chart before and after change in treatment guidelines.

mean in the desired direction and a decrease in the amount of variation. Both of these are evident in the side-by-side inspection of the data sets.

Figure 10.16 evaluates the process performance *after* the change in treatment guidelines, as measured by both the TTG ratio and sigma level. The TTG ratio is now 71.4 percent (20 of 28 INR readings are within the 2.5 to 3.5 SLs), which translates into a 2.1 sigma level of performance.

Figure 10.17 is a specification chart of the process after the change in treatment guidelines. Both Figure 10.16 and 10.17 tell the same story. The process capability in Figure 10.16 as measured by the TTG ratio is 20/28, or 71.4 percent.

N	D	DPMO	M	TTG	NTTG	SIGMA

enter numerator (# NTTG) and denominator (# total) in the appropriate fields

| | Numerator: | 8 | | | Denominator: | 28 | |

N	D	DPMO	M	TTG	NTTG	SIGMA
PERFORMANCE						
8	28	285714	1000000	71.43%	28.57%	2.1

Figure 10.16 Evaluation of anticoagulation process after change in treatment guidelines.

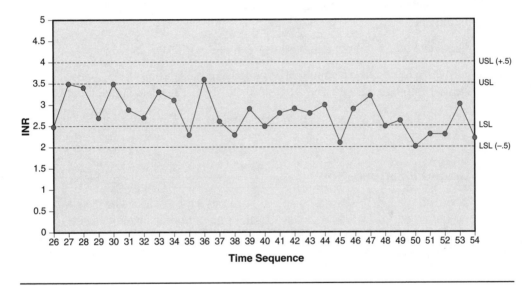

Figure 10.17 Anticoagulation specification chart after process change.

In Figure 10.17, observe what happens if the specification limits are moved + and − 0.5. Figure 10.17 shows that the assessment of process capability as measured by the TTG ratio improves from 71.4 percent to 100 percent.

After the process change there were no further episodes of bleeding and no TIAs or strokes in this patient. The internists became confident enough in self-measurement to give some of their patients an INR specification chart and allowed them access to pro-thrombin time and INR lab reports on the day of service, which they chart and bring to their physicians at the time of their follow-up visits. This patient has standing orders for modification of Warfarin dosage. Both the patient and the physician learned to retest the INR, not to change the dose of Warfarin. The patient calls his physician proactively when the INR is more than ±0.5 beyond nationally accepted control limits.

CASE STUDY #3: DIABETIC PATIENT WITH HYPERTENSION

The Situation

A 58-year-old man with diabetes mellitus presents with hypertension. American Diabetes Association guidelines[7] suggest that blood pressure (BP) in diabetics should be aggressively treated to systolic ≤ 130 and diastolic ≤ 85. The data for this case are found in Table 10.6. The systolic BP data are analyzed in the control chart in Figure 10.18. The diastolic BP data are analyzed in the control chart in Figure 10.19.

Questions

1. Were 16 BP readings adequate to establish a baseline for evaluating treatment?

2. What can be said about response to treatment with ACE inhibitors?

3. Did the addition of a second antihypertensive medication (beta blockers) further improve the process?

4. What is the process capability as measured by the TTG ratio for the last process of care?

Analysis and Interpretation

1. There are two KOVs: systolic and diastolic blood pressure. The baseline measurement of 16 readings was less than the 20 points (or subgroups) that are desired to evaluate process stability with confidence. (This issue was discussed in chapter 2.) However, the minimal variation and narrow control limits observed in the baseline measurement of both systolic and diastolic BP (Figures 10.18 and 10.19) provided reasonable assurance that the process was stable and predictable, although certainly unacceptable. The mean baseline BP for both the systolic and diastolic readings was above their respective specification limits (SLs) of 130 and 85.

2. The initial treatment with ACE inhibitors at time sequence (TS) 17 was effective in reducing both the systolic BP and the diastolic BP, as demonstrated by the special cause in both measurements.[8] However, while the mean diastolic BP dropped below the SL of 85, the mean systolic BP continued to be above its SL of 130.

3. When beta blockers were added to ACE inhibitors at time 24, both the systolic and diastolic readings dropped even further. The systolic process now averaged 127, and only two of the last 14 readings were above the SL of 130. The diastolic BP readings now averaged 69.7, and all of the last 14 readings were below the SL of 85.

4. After the beta blockers were prescribed along with the ACE inhibitors, the TTG ratio for the systolic readings was 79 percent (11/13). The TTG ratio for diastolic BP was 100 percent (all the 14 readings were below 85).

Table 10.6   Blood pressure data set for diabetic patient.

PN	Visit	TS	Sys BP	Dia BP	Pulse	Weight	E&M	Rx
10041	3/18/1999	1	180	98	92	170	99213	no bp med
10041	3/22/1999	2	196	100	72	172	99215	no bp med
10041	3/26/1999	3	184	96	92	166	99213	no bp med
10041	3/30/1999	4	186	98	80	168	99213	no bp med
10041	4/3/1999	5	198	94	80	164	99213	no bp med
10041	4/7/1999	6	188	95	72	166	99213	no bp med
10041	4/11/1999	7	180	99	60	167	99213	no bp med
10041	4/15/1999	8	192	100	80	167	99213	no bp med
10041	4/19/1999	9	194	98	60	161	99213	no bp med
10041	4/23/1999	10	188	94	72	159	99213	no bp med
10041	4/27/1999	11	194	96	74	162	99213	no bp med
10041	5/1/1999	12	186	98	80	160	99213	no bp med
10041	5/5/1999	13	184	102	72	160	99213	no bp med
10041	5/9/1999	14	192	96	90	159	99213	no bp med
10041	5/13/1999	15	186	95	74	160	99213	no bp med
10041	5/17/1999	16	184	98	92	160	99213	no bp med
10041	6/12/1999	17	128	72	72	160	99213	ACE
10041	7/7/1999	18	152	86	72	162	99213	ACE
10041	8/26/1999	19	150	64	72	166	99213	ACE
10041	9/1/1999	20	138	68	80	155	99213	ACE
10041	9/3/1999	21	146	86	68	162	99213	ACE
10041	9/7/1999	22	158	74	92	164	99213	ACE
10041	10/19/1999	23	160	78	72	162	99213	ACE
10041	11/22/1999	24	128	72	80	166	99213	ACE & BB
10041	12/28/1999	25	120	58	70	159	99213	ACE & BB
10041	1/10/2000	26	128	68	70	151	99213	ACE & BB
10041	1/24/2000	27	130	72	68	152	99213	ACE & BB
10041	3/15/2000	28	125	74	78	151	99213	ACE & BB
10041	4/19/2000	29	126	68	82	153	99213	ACE & BB
10041	5/17/2000	30	124	70	74	150	99213	ACE & BB
10041	7/15/2000	31	128	72	82	151	99213	ACE & BB
10041	8/16/2000	32	134	82	80	152	99213	ACE & BB
10041	10/26/2000	33	134	76	82	158	99213	ACE & BB
10041	11/8/2000	34	128	60	78	156	99213	ACE & BB
10041	11/23/2000	35	122	64	80	157	99213	ACE & BB
10041	12/21/2000	36	124	58	64	155	99213	ACE & BB
10041	12/30/2000	37	130	82	90	158	99213	ACE & BB

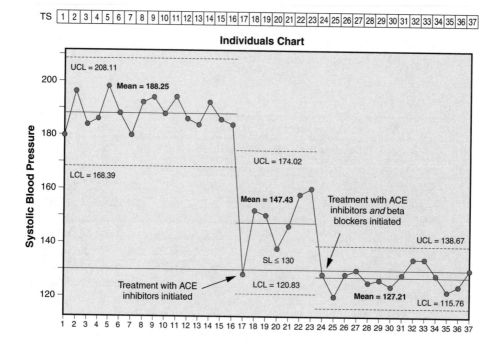

Figure 10.18 Systolic blood pressure—diabetic patient with hypertension.

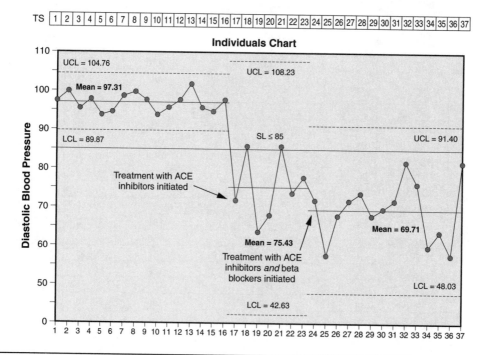

Figure 10.19 Diastolic blood pressure—diabetic patient with hypertension.

THE USE OF CONTROL CHARTS IN CLINICAL MEDICINE

Specification charts have been used in manufacturing in the United States since the days of the Civil War. Control charts were developed at Bell Laboratories by Shewhart in the 1920s, and were widely promoted and used by Deming and Juran in their work in support of manufacturing in postwar Japan. It is accurate to say that statistical process control—including control charting—has been a part of engineering and manufacturing in this country for over 50 years. However, the mathematics and science of this discipline have been late in coming to clinical medicine. In a way this is fortunate, because the methods are so precise that they sometimes appear of little utility when applied to biological systems with interrelated complex mechanisms that seem to run autonomously. Control charts in medicine have been talked about, but not widely used.

While Deming[9] referenced the work of Hirokawa and Sugiyama,[10] who were on the engineering faculty at Osaka University in Japan and had in 1980 used X-bar and R-charts to follow the progress of patients learning to walk after an operation, Laffel and Blumenthal[11] were perhaps the earliest medical writers who recognized the value of control charts in clinical medicine. Roberts[12] suggested the use of control charts to monitor prevention of athletic training injuries, diabetes, and smoking cessation and gave an example of control charts used to monitor blood pressure (pages 148–154). Carey and Lloyd[13] provide several case studies of the use of control charts at the macrosystems level related to laboratory turnaround time, caesarian section rate, patient falls, use of restraints, and medication errors. However, they also included two case studies on the use of control charts for individual patient care: measuring the progress of physical therapy and measuring platelet counts. Nelson et al.[14] give examples of the use of control charts in individual clinical care and in monitoring length of stay, time to therapy, and duration of therapy for community-acquired pneumonia. Gibson et al.[15] report the use of control charts to help physicians understand the degree of variability in individual asthma patients' peak expiratory flow rates. The analysis of the control charts in this case enabled physicians and patients to work together to individualize care plans and manage asthma exacerbation at an earlier stage. Boggs[16] also makes a strong case for the use of control charts in clinical care of patients with asthma. Several clinicians have reported on the use of control charts to respond appropriately to variation in blood sugar readings for diabetics.[17–20] Laffel et al.[21] analyzed continuous data streams from ICU patients that suggest that physicians may be overmedicating patients in response to random variation in readings. Benneyan[22–26] has given careful thought to the creation of new control charts, called "g" and "h" charts, specifically suited for monitoring change over time where infrequent adverse events in the numerator are very small compared with the denominator. In the future, the use of several types of control charts for monitoring error rates and changing physiological and laboratory variables promises to be particularly fruitful.

The use of control charts continues to be on the agenda of the Institute of Healthcare Improvement, a Boston-based group promoting quality improvement in healthcare, and is a key part of their annual meetings, called the National Forum. The National Committee on Quality Assurance (NCQA), Washington, DC, has also taken the initiative to promote the use of control charts in meeting HEDIS standards and objectives. The Joint Commission on Accreditation of Healthcare Organizations (Oakbrook Terrace, Illinois) has used control charts as part of their survey process since 2000.

There is a real need for guidelines and standardization in the use of these tools in clinical medicine. When should we be using two-sigma or three-sigma control charts in clinical care? How should we set specification limits for various diseases? What are community performance standards and levels? Are these levels good enough? And as Dr. Mark Chassin[27] asked a few years ago, "Is medicine really ready for Six Sigma?"

SUMMARY

The clinical examples in diabetes, coronary artery disease, and anticoagulation presented in this chapter demonstrate three tools for display of time sequence data: line charts with specification limits, run charts, and control charts. Baseline data are always necessary and can be provided for population studies with histograms and for both population and individual studies with control charts. The tools can also be mixed and matched. It is possible to superimpose specification limits on a run chart or on a control chart, though the simplicity of the original charts is somewhat compromised. Simple methods for estimating process capability have been introduced that are useful for understanding defect rates and setting goals for defect rate reduction.

ENDNOTES

1. R. J. Rubin, W. M. Altman, and D. N. Mendelson, "Health Care Expenditures for People with Diabetes Mellitus, 1992," *Journal of Clinical Endocrinology and Metabolism* 78, no. 4 (April 1994): 809A–F.

2. I intend to add to the discussion of "process capability" in Chapter 4.

3. Baseline population analysis in 2000 would not be quite so striking because Metformin and Thiazoladinediones (TZDs) are now widely used and have had an impressive impact on HbA1c. See Group, D.C.A.T.R. (1993); Group, U.K.P.D.S. (1998a), and Group, U.K.P.D.S. (1998b)

4. S. M. Zimmerman and M. L. Icenogle, *Statistical Quality Control Using Excel* (Milwaukee: ASQ Quality Press, 1999).

5. The reader may wish to refer back to chapter 2 to review the basic elements of a control chart, the control chart decision tree, and the tests for a special cause.

6. T. R. Pedersen, et al., "Randomized Trial of Cholesterol Lowering in 4,444 Patients with Coronary Heart Disease: The Scandinavian Simvastatin Survival Study (4S), *Lancet* 344 (1994): 1383–89.

7. American Diabetes Association, "Clinical Practice Recommendations 2000," *Diabetes Care* 23, Supplement 1 (2000): S1–S116.

8. Ordinarily eight points below the previous mean would be required for a special cause, but in this instance the shift was very evident with only seven points.

9. W. E. Deming, *Out of the Crisis* (Cambridge, MA: MIT Center for Advanced Engineering Studies, 1982): 252–53.

10. S. Hirokawa and H. Sugiyama, "Quantitative Gain Analysis," *Technology Reports of Osaka University, Faculty of Engineering* 30 (1980): 1520.

11. G. Laffel and D. Blumenthal, "The Case for Using Industrial Quality Management Science in Health Care Organizations," *Journal of the American Medical Association* 262, no. 20 (1989): 2869–73.

12. H. V. Roberts and B. F. Sergesketter, *Quality is Personal: A Foundation for Total Quality Management* (New York: The Free Press, 1993): 148–54.

13. R. G. Carey and R. C. Lloyd, *Measuring Quality Improvement in Healthcare: A Guide to Statistical Process Control Applications* (Milwaukee: ASQ Quality Press, 2001).

14. E. C. Nelson, et al., "Building Measurement and Data Collection onto Medical Practice," *Annals of Internal Medicine* 128 (1998): 460–66.

15. P. G. Gibson, et al., "Using Quality-Control Analysis of Peak Expiratory Flow Recordings to Guide Therapy for Asthma," *Annals of Internal Medicine* 123 (1995): 488–92.

16. P. Boggs, "Peak Expiratory Flow Rate Control Chart: A Breakthrough in Asthma Care," *Annals of Allergy, Asthma, and Immunology* 77 (1996): 423–29.

17. Nelson, "Building measurement and data collection," 460–66.

18. E. C. Nelson, P. B. Batalden, and J. C. Reyer, *Clinical Improvement Action Guide,* ed. E. C. Nelson (Chicago: Joint Commission on Accreditation of Healthcare Organizations, 1997).

19. T. A. Oniki, et al., "Using Statistical Quality Control Techniques to Monitor Blood Glucose Levels," proceedings of the Annual Symposium on Computer Applications in Medical Care (1995).

20. L. V. Staker, "Putting More Quality into Practice: Statistical Process Control and Diabetes," in *ENH Outcomes Management Conference* (Evanston, IL: Evanston Northwestern Healthcare, 1998): 586–90.

21. G. Laffel, R. Luttman, and S. Zimmerman, "Using Control Charts to Analyze Serial Patient-Related Data," *Quality Management in Health Care* 3, no. 1 (1994): 70–77.

22. J. C. Benneyan, Statistical Control Charts Based on Geometric and Negative Binomial Populations (University of Massachusetts: Amhurst, Massachusetts, 1992).

23. J. C. Benneyan, "Use and Interpretation of Statistical Quality Control Charts," *International Journal of Quality Health Care* 10, no. 1 (1998): 69–73.

24. J. C. Benneyan, "Statistical Process Control in Infection Control and Epidemiology (Part 1)," *Infection Control and Hospital Epidemiology* 19, no. 3 (1998): 194–214.

25. J. C. Benneyan, "Statistical Process Control in Infection Control and Epidemiology (Part 2)," *Infection Control and Hospital Epidemiology* 19, no. 4 (1998): 265–83.

26. J. C. Benneyan, "Geometric g-Type Statistical Control Charts for Infrequent Adverse Events," in *IEE Social Health Systems Proceedings* (1999).

27. M. Chassin, "Is Health Care Ready for Six Sigma Quality?" *The Milbank Quarterly* 76, no. 4 (1998): 565–91.

Appendix

SPC Software and the Formulas for Calculating Control Limits

SOFTWARE PACKAGES

The following software packages are among the most commonly used by various healthcare organizations. Other software packages are also listed periodically in *Quality Progress* (published by ASQ, Milwaukee, Wisconsin).

CHARTrunner 2000 Version 1.5

- Owned by PQ Systems, Miamisburg, Ohio
- Obtain free trial download at www.chartrunner.com
- Call 800-777-3020 for information

Minitab

- Associated with Penn State University
- For free demo software, call 800-448-3555

QI Analyst Version 3.5

- Owned by Wonderware, Lake Forest, California
- Contact Kelly.kunkle@wonderware.com

QI Macros

- Owned by LifeStar, Denver, Colorado
- For information, call 888-468-1535

Quality America

- For information, call 800-248-1753
- E-mail: sales@qualityamerica.com

Statit

- Sold by Statware, Corvallis, Oregon
- For information, call 800-478-2892
- E-mail: info@statware.com

FORMULAS FOR CALCULATING CONTROL LIMITS

The formulas for all the control charts used in this volume—with the exception of the X-bar and S-chart—can be found in Carey and Lloyd (2001), on pages 183–186 of the appendix.

The formula for the X-bar and S-chart, including the list of the numerical constants, can be found in the appendix of Wheeler's (1995) text, Table 10, page 425.

References

American Diabetes Association, "Clinical Practice Recommendations 2000." *Diabetes Care* 23, Supplement 1 (2000): S1–S116.

American Society for Testing and Materials. *Manual on Presentation of Data and Control Chart Analysis.* 6th ed. Philadelphia: American Society for Testing and Materials, 1995.

Babbie, E. *The Practice of Social Research.* 8th ed. New York: Wadsworth, 1998.

Ballestracci, D. and J. L. Barlow. *Quality Improvement: Practical Applications for Medical Group Practice.* 2nd ed. Englewood, CO: Center for Research in Ambulatory Health Care Administration, 1996.

Benneyan, J. C. *Statistical Control Charts Based on Geometric and Negative Binomial Populations.* (Amherst, MA: University of Massachusetts): 1992.

———. "Use and Interpretation of Statistical Quality Control Charts." *International Journal of Quality Health Care* 10, no. 1 (1998a): 69–73.

———. "Statistical Process Control in Infection Control and Epidemiology (Part 1)" *Infection Control and Hospital Epidemiology* 19, no. 3 (1998b): 194–214.

———. "Statistical Process Control in Infection Control and Epidemiology (Part 2)" *Infection Control and Hospital Epidemiology* 19, no. 4 (1998c): 265–83.

———. "Geometric g-Type Statistical Control Charts for Infrequent Adverse Events" in *IIE Social Health Systems Proceedings* (1999).

Boggs, P. "Peak Expiratory Flow Rate Control Chart: A Breakthrough in Asthma Care." *Annals of Allergy, Asthma, and Immunology* 77 (1996): 423–29.

Brook, R. H., C. J. Kamberg, and E. A. McGlynn. "Health System Reform and Quality." *Journal of the American Medical Association* 276, no. 6 (14 August 1996): 476.

Byers, J. F. and C L. Beaudin. "The Relationship between Continuous Quality Improvement and Research." *Journal of Healthcare Quality* (January/February 2002): 4–8.

Camp, R. *Benchmarking: The Search for Industry Best Practices That Lead to Superior Performance.* Milwaukee: ASQC Quality Press, 1989.

Carey, R. G. "How to Choose a Patient Survey System." *Joint Commission Journal on Quality Improvement* 25, no. 1 (January 1999): 20–25.

Carey, R. G. and J. H. Seibert. "A Patient Survey System to Measure Quality Improvement: Questionnaire Validity and Reliability." *Medical Care* 31 (1993): 834–945.

Carey, R. G. and R. C. Lloyd. *Measuring Quality Improvement in Healthcare: A Guide to Statistical Process Control Applications.* Milwaukee: ASQ Quality Press, 2001.

Casarett, D., J. H. Karlawish, and J. Sugarman. "Determining When Quality Improvement Initiatives Should Be Considered Research: Proposed Criteria and Potential Implications." *Journal of the American Medical Association* 283, no. 17 (2000): 2275–80.

Chassin, M. "Is Health Care Ready for Six Sigma Quality?" *The Milbank Quarterly* 76, no. 4 (1998): 565–91.

Chow, C. W. et al. "The Balanced Scorecard: A Potent Tool for Energizing and Focusing Healthcare Organization Management." *Journal of Healthcare Management* 43, no. 3, (May/June 1998): 263–80.

Deming, W. E. *Out of the Crisis*. Cambridge, MA: MIT Center for Advanced Engineering Studies, 1982.

————. *The New Economics*. 2nd ed. Boston: MIT Center for Advanced Engineering Study, 1994.

Duncan, A. J. *Quality Control and Industrial Statistics*. Homewood, IL: Irwin, 1986.

Erwin, J. "Achieving Total Customer Satisfaction through Six Sigma." *Quality Digest* (July 1998): 38–42.

Gibson, P. G., et al. "Using Quality-Control Analysis of Peak Expiratory Flow Recordings to Guide Therapy for Asthma." *Annals of Internal Medicine* 123 (1995): 488–92.

Graham, J. D. and M. J. Cleary, eds. *Practical Tools for Continuous Improvement*. Vol. 1. Miamisburg, OH: PQ Systems, 2000.

Grant, E. L. and R. S. Leavenworth. *Statistical Quality Control*. New York: McGraw-Hill, 1988.

Group, D.C.a.C.T.R. "The Effect of Intensive Treatment of Diabetes on the Development and Progression of Long-Term Complications in Insulin-Dependent Diabetes Mellitus." *New England Journal of Medicine* 329 (1993): 977–86.

Group, U.K.P.D.S. "Intensive Blood-Glucose Control with Sulphonylureas or Insulin Compared with Conventional Treatment and Risk of Complications in Patients with Type 2 Diabetes (UKPDS 33)." *The Lancet* 352, no. 9131 (1998): 837–53.

————. "Effect of Intensive Blood-Glucose Control with Metformin on Complications in Overweight Patients with Type 2 Diabetes (UKPDS 34)." *The Lancet* 352 no. 9131 (1998): 854–65.

Harry, M. and R. Schroeder. *Six Sigma*. New York: Currency, 2000.

Hart, M. K. and R. F. Hart. *Statistical Process Control for Health Care*. Pacific Grove, CA: Duxbury, 2002.

Hayes, B. E. *Measuring Customer Satisfaction*. Milwaukee: ASQ Quality Press, 1997.

Hirokawa, S. and H. Sugiyama. "Quantitative Gain Analysis." *Technology Reports of Osaka University, Faculty of Engineering* 30, no. 1520 (1980).

Kaplan, R. S. and D. P. Norton. "Using the Balanced Scorecard As a Strategic Management System." *Harvard Business Review*. (January–February, 1996): 75–85.

Laffel, G. and D. Blumenthal. "The Case for Using Industrial Quality Management Science in Health Care Organizations. *Journal of the American Medical Association* 262, no. 20 (1989): 2869–73.

Laffel, G., R. Luttman, and S. Zimmerman. "Using Control Charts to Analyze Serial Patient-Related Data." *Quality Management in Health Care* 3, no. 1 (1994): 70–77.

Langley, G. J., et al. *The Improvement Guide*. San Francisco: Jossey-Bass, 1996.

Lawton, R. "Balance Your Balanced Scorecard." *ASQ Quality Progress* (March 2002): 66–71.

Lee, K. and C. McGreevey. "Using Control Charts to Assess Performance Measurement Data. *Journal on Quality Improvement*. 28, no. 2 (February 2002): 90–101.

————. "Using Comparison Charts to Assess Performance Measurement Data." *Journal on Quality Improvement* 28, no. 3 (March 2002): 129–138.

Moen, R. D., T. W. Nolan, and L. P. Provost. *Quality Improvement through Planned Experimentation.* New York: McGraw-Hill, 1999.

Montgomery, D. C. *Introduction to Statistical Quality Control.* New York: John Wiley & Sons, 1991.

Nelson, E. C., et al. Building Measurement and Data Collection into Medical Practice. *Annals of Internal Medicine* 128 (1998): 460–66.

Nelson, E. C., P. B. Batalden, and J. C. Reyer. *Clinical Improvement Action Guide*, ed. E. C. Nelson. Chicago: Joint Commission on Accreditation of Healthcare Organizations, 1997.

Oniki, T. A., et al., "Using Statistical Quality Control Techniques to Monitor Blood Glucose Levels." Proceedings of the Annual Symposium on Computer Applications in Medical Care, 1995.

Pedersen, T. R., et al. "Randomized Trial of Cholesterol Lowering in 4,444 Patients with Coronary Heart Disease: The Scandinavian Simvastatin Survival Study (4S)." *The Lancet* 344 (1994): 1383–89.

Pyzdek, T. *Pyzdek's Guide to SPC.* Vol. 1. Tucson, AZ: Quality Publishing, 1990.

———. *Pyzdek's Guide to SPC.* Vol. 2. Tucson, AZ: Quality Publishing, 1992.

———. *The Complete Guide to Six Sigma.* Tucson, AZ: Quality Publishing, 1999.

Ramburg, J. S. "Six Sigma: Fad or Fundamental?" *Quality Digest* (May 2000): 28–37.

Roberts, H. V. and B. F. Sergesketter. *Quality Is Personal: A Foundation for Total Quality Management.* New York: The Free Press, 1993, 169.

Rubin, R. J., W. M. Altman, and D. N. Mendelson. "Health Care Expenditures for People with Diabetes Mellitus, 1992." *Journal of Clinical Endocrinology and Metabolism* 78, no.4 (April 1994): 809A–F.

Seibert, J. H., J. M. Strohmeyer, and R. G. Carey, "Evaluating the Physician Office Visit: In Pursuit of a Valid and Reliable Measure of Quality Improvement Efforts." *Journal of Ambulatory Care Management* 19, no. 1 (1996): 17–37.

Shewhart, W. A. *Economic Control of Quality of Manufactured Product.* New York: Van Nostrand, 1931.

Snee, R. D. "Why Should Statisticians Pay Attention to Six Sigma?" *ASQ Quality Progress* (September 1999).

Solberg, L., G. Mosser, and S. McDonald. "The Three Faces of Performance Measurement: Improvement, Accountability, and Research." *Journal on Quality Improvement* 23, no. 3, (March 1997): 135.

Staker, L. V. "Putting More Quality into Practice: Statistical Process Control and Diabetes." In *ENH Outcomes Management Conference.* Evanston, IL: Evanston Northwestern Healthcare, (1998): 586–90.

Sweed, F., and C. Eisenhart. "Tables for Testing Randomness of Groupings in a Sequence of Alternatives." In *Annals of Mathematical Statistics.* Vol. XIV (1943): 66–87.

Western Electric Company. *Statistical Quality Control Handbook.* Indianapolis: AT&T Technologies, 1984.

Wheeler, D. J. *Advanced Topics in Statistical Process Control.* Knoxville, TN: SPC Press, 1995.

Wheeler, D. J., and D. S. Chambers. *Understanding Statistical Process Control.* Knoxville, TN: SPC Press, 1992.

Zimmerman, S. M., and M. L. Icenogle, *Statistical Quality Control Using Excel.* Milwaukee: ASQ Quality Press, 1999.

About the Authors

Principal author: Raymond G. Carey, PhD

As principal of R. G. Carey and Associates (Park Ridge, Illinois), Dr. Carey conducts national and international seminars on the use of statistical process control methodology for improving healthcare. He was formerly vice president of quality measurement at Lutheran General Hospital/Advocate (Park Ridge, Illinois), and president of Parkside Associates. Since 1999, he has served as a member of the Joint Commission's Advisory Council on Performance Measurement.

Dr. Carey received his doctorate in social psychology from Loyola University of Chicago. He has published over 50 articles and several books. He has also co-authored two books: *Program Evaluation,* an internationally recognized textbook in evaluation research; and *Measuring Quality Improvement in Healthcare: A Guide to Statistical Process Control Applications.*

Internationally, he has presented seminars on statistical process control to leading Austrian physicians and administrators at the University of Vienna Business School; to the Calgary Regional Health Authority in Alberta, Canada; to the Federation of County Councils in Stockholm, Sweden; and to the Health Authority in Fabriano, Italy.

Guest author of Chapter 10: Larry V. Staker, MD, FACP

Dr. Staker is a national lecturer on healthcare quality, especially on the application of the principles of improvement in the day-to-day care of patients. He is currently chief medical officer and medical director for Deseret Mutual (Salt Lake City, Utah). In addition to maintaining his practice in general internal medicine, he is associate professor of medicine at the University of Utah College of Medicine (Salt Lake City).

From 1986 to 1994 he was part of a large group practice at Bryner Clinic in Salt Lake City. After Bryner Clinic was integrated into Intermountain Health Care in 1995, Dr. Staker served as director of clinical practice improvement and chairman of the quality committee for the physician division until 1999.

After graduating from medical school at the University of Utah in Salt Lake City in 1968, Dr. Staker did his residency in internal medicine at the National Naval Medical Center (Bethesda, Maryland). Later he was full-time faculty in the Division of General Medicine at the University of Utah Health Science Center from 1984 to 1989.

Index